Gather Together

Publications International, Ltd.

Some of the products listed in this publication may be in limited distribution.

Pictured on the front cover: Spaghetti & Meatballs *(page 110)*. Photograph on cover © Shutterstock.com

Pictured on the back cover *(clockwise left to right)*: Bruschetta *(page 5)*, Chicken Noodle Soup *(page 51)*, and Smashed Potatoes *(page 141)*.

ISBN: 978-1-64030-725-4

Manufactured in China.

8 7 6 5 4 3 2 1

Microwave Cooking: Microwave ovens vary in wattage. Use the cooking times as guidelines and check for doneness before adding more time.

Let's get social!

⊙ @Publications_International

f @PublicationsInternational

www.pilcookbooks.com

Bruschetta (page 5) Creamy Tomato Soup (page 52) Garlic Knots (page 146)

Contents

Appetizers

Bruschetta

4 plum tomatoes, seeded and diced

½ cup packed fresh basil leaves, finely chopped

5 tablespoons olive oil, divided

2 cloves garlic, minced

2 teaspoons finely chopped oil-packed sun-dried tomatoes

¼ teaspoon salt

⅛ teaspoon black pepper

16 slices Italian bread

2 tablespoons grated Parmesan cheese (optional)

1 Combine fresh tomatoes, basil, 3 tablespoons oil, garlic, sun-dried tomatoes, salt and pepper in large bowl; mix well. Let stand at room temperature 1 hour to blend flavors.

2 Preheat oven to 375°F. Place bread on baking sheet. Brush remaining 2 tablespoons oil over one side of each bread slice; sprinkle with cheese, if desired. Bake 6 to 8 minutes or until toasted.

3 Top each bread slice with 1 tablespoon tomato mixture.

Makes 1 cup (8 servings)

Apricot Brie En Croûte

1 sheet frozen puff pastry (half of 17¼-ounce package)

1 round (8 ounces) Brie cheese

¼ cup apricot preserves

1 Unfold puff pastry; thaw 20 minutes on lightly floured surface. Preheat oven to 400°F. Line baking sheet with parchment paper.

2 Roll out puff pastry to 12-inch square. Place Brie in center of square; spread preserves over top of Brie.

3 Gather up edges of puff pastry; bring together over center of Brie, covering cheese entirely. Pinch and twist pastry edges together to seal. Transfer to prepared baking sheet.

4 Bake 20 to 25 minutes or until golden brown. (If top of pastry browns too quickly, cover loosely with small piece of foil.) Serve warm.

Makes 6 servings

Variation: For added flavor and texture, sprinkle 2 tablespoons sliced almonds over the preserves. Proceed with wrapping and baking the Brie as directed.

Guacamole

Corn Tortilla Chips (recipe follows) or packaged corn tortilla chips

4 tablespoons finely chopped white onion, divided

1 to 2 serrano or jalapeño peppers,* seeded and finely chopped

1½ tablespoons coarsely chopped fresh cilantro, divided

¼ teaspoon chopped garlic (optional)

2 large ripe avocados

1 medium tomato, peeled and chopped

1 to 2 teaspoons fresh lime juice

¼ teaspoon salt

Serrano and jalapeño peppers can sting and irritate the skin, so wear rubber gloves when handling peppers and do not touch your eyes.

1 Prepare Corn Tortilla Chips.

2 Combine 2 tablespoons onion, serrano pepper, 1 tablespoon cilantro and garlic, if desired, in large mortar. Grind with pestle until almost smooth. (Mixture can be processed in food processor, if necessary, but it may become more watery than desired.)

3 Cut avocados into halves; remove and discard pits. Scoop out pulp; place in large bowl. Add pepper mixture; mash roughly, leaving avocado slightly chunky.

4 Add tomato, lime juice, salt, remaining 2 tablespoons onion and ½ tablespoon cilantro to avocado mixture; mix well. Serve immediately with Corn Tortilla Chips or cover and refrigerate up to 4 hours.

Makes about 2 cups

Corn Tortilla Chips

12 (6-inch) corn tortillas, day-old*

Vegetable oil

½ to 1 teaspoon salt

If tortillas are fresh, let stand, uncovered, in single layer on wire rack 1 to 2 hours to dry slightly.

1 Stack 6 tortillas. Cutting through stack, cut into 6 equal wedges. Repeat with remaining tortillas.

2 Heat ½ inch oil in large heavy skillet over medium-high heat to 375°F; adjust heat to maintain temperature.

3 Fry tortilla wedges in single layer 1 minute or until crisp, turning occasionally. Remove and drain on paper towels. Sprinkle chips with salt. Repeat with remaining wedges.

Makes 6 dozen

Tip: Tortilla chips are served with salsa, used as the base for nachos and used as scoops for guacamole, refried beans or other dips. They are best eaten fresh, but can be stored, tightly covered, in cool place 2 to 3 days. Reheat in 350°F oven a few minutes before serving.

Cocktail Meatballs

1 pound ground beef

1 pound bulk pork or
   Italian sausage

1 cup plain dry bread
   crumbs

1 cup finely chopped
   onion

1 cup finely chopped
   green bell pepper

½ cup milk

1 egg, beaten

2 teaspoons salt

1 teaspoon Italian
   seasoning

¼ teaspoon black pepper

1 cup ketchup

¾ cup packed brown
   sugar

½ cup (1 stick) butter

½ cup cider vinegar

¼ cup water

¼ cup lemon juice

1 teaspoon yellow
   mustard

¼ teaspoon garlic salt

Slow Cooker Directions

1 Preheat oven to 350°F. Combine beef, sausage, bread crumbs, onion, bell pepper, milk, egg, salt, Italian seasoning and black pepper in large bowl; mixing lightly but thoroughly. Shape mixture into 1-inch balls. Place meatballs on racks on two nonstick baking sheets. Bake 25 minutes or until meatballs are browned.

2 Meanwhile, place ketchup, brown sugar, butter, vinegar, water, lemon juice, mustard and garlic salt in 4-quart slow cooker; mix well. Cover; cook on HIGH until hot.

3 Transfer meatballs to slow cooker; carefully stir to coat with sauce. Turn slow cooker to LOW. Cover; cook 2 hours.

Makes 12 servings

Soy-Braised Chicken Wings

¼ cup dry sherry

¼ cup soy sauce

3 tablespoons sugar

2 tablespoons cornstarch

2 tablespoons minced garlic, divided

2 teaspoons red pepper flakes

12 chicken wings (about 2½ pounds), tips removed, split at joints

2 tablespoons vegetable oil

3 green onions, cut into 1-inch pieces

¼ cup chicken broth

1 teaspoon dark sesame oil

1 tablespoon sesame seeds, toasted

To toast sesame seeds, place in small skillet. Shake skillet over medium-low heat about 3 minutes or until seeds begin to pop and turn golden. Remove from heat.

Slow Cooker Directions

1 Combine sherry, soy sauce, sugar, cornstarch, 1 tablespoon garlic and red pepper flakes in large bowl; mix well. Reserve ¼ cup marinade in separate bowl. Stir wings into remaining marinade. Cover; marinate in refrigerator overnight, turning once or twice.

2 Drain wings; discard marinade. Heat 1 tablespoon vegetable oil in wok or large skillet over high heat 1 minute. Add half of wings; cook 3 to 4 minutes or until wings are browned on all sides, turning occasionally. Remove with slotted spoon to slow cooker. Repeat with remaining vegetable oil and wings.

3 Add remaining 1 tablespoon garlic and green onions to wok; cook and stir 30 seconds. Stir in broth; pour over wings. Cover; cook on HIGH 2 hours or until wings are cooked through.

4 Add sesame oil to reserved marinade; mix well. Pour over wings; sprinkle with sesame seeds. Serve immediately.

Makes 2 dozen wings

Mozzarella Sticks

¼ cup all-purpose flour

2 eggs

1 tablespoon water

1 cup plain dry bread crumbs

2 teaspoons Italian seasoning

½ teaspoon salt

½ teaspoon garlic powder

1 package (12 ounces) string cheese (12 sticks)

Vegetable oil for frying

1 cup marinara or pizza sauce, heated

1 Place flour in shallow bowl. Whisk eggs and water in another shallow bowl. Combine bread crumbs, Italian seasoning, salt and garlic powder in third shallow bowl.

2 Coat each piece of cheese with flour. Dip in egg mixture, letting excess drip back into bowl. Roll in bread crumb mixture to coat. Dip again in egg mixture and roll again in bread crumb mixture. Refrigerate until ready to cook.

3 Heat 2 inches of oil in large saucepan over medium-high heat to 350°F; adjust heat to maintain temperature. Add cheese sticks; cook about 1 minute or until golden brown. Drain on wire rack. Serve with warm marinara sauce for dipping.

Makes 4 to 6 servings

Salsa

1 can (28 ounces) whole
   Italian plum tomatoes,
   undrained

2 fresh plum tomatoes,
   seeded and coarsely
   chopped

2 tablespoons canned
   diced mild green chiles

1 tablespoon canned
   diced jalapeño
   peppers (optional)

1 tablespoon white
   vinegar

1 clove garlic, minced

1 teaspoon onion powder

1 teaspoon sugar

1 teaspoon ground cumin

½ teaspoon garlic powder

¼ teaspoon salt

   Tortilla chips

1 Combine tomatoes with juice, fresh tomatoes, green
chiles, jalapeño peppers, if desired, vinegar, garlic, onion
powder, sugar, cumin, garlic powder and salt in food
processor; process until finely chopped.

2 Serve with tortilla chips.

Makes 4½ cups

Buffalo Chicken Dip

2 packages (8 ounces each) cream cheese, softened and cut into pieces

1 jar (12 ounces) restaurant-style wing sauce

1 cup ranch dressing

2 cups shredded cooked chicken (from 1 pound boneless skinless chicken breasts)

2 cups (8 ounces) shredded Cheddar cheese

Tortilla chips

Celery sticks

1 Combine cream cheese, wing sauce and ranch dressing in large saucepan; cook over medium-low heat 7 to 10 minutes or until cream cheese is melted and mixture is smooth, whisking frequently.

2 Combine chicken and Cheddar cheese in large bowl. Add cream cheese mixture; stir until well blended. Pour into serving bowl; serve warm with tortilla chips and celery sticks.

Makes 5 cups

Asian Chicken Meatballs with Spicy Cucumber Salad

Sauce

¼ cup hoisin sauce

3 tablespoons unseasoned rice vinegar

1 tablespoon soy sauce

1 teaspoon fresh grated ginger

2 cloves garlic, crushed

Cucumber Salad

¼ cup rice vinegar

2 teaspoons sugar

6 mini cucumbers, thinly slice

½ red onion, thinly sliced

½ jalapeño pepper,* seeded and finely chopped

2 tablespoons chopped fresh cilantro

Meatballs

½ cup uncooked quinoa

1 cup water

1 pound ground chicken

1 egg

1 teaspoon fresh grated ginger

1 teaspoon dark sesame oil

¼ cup thinly sliced green onions (about 2)

2 cloves garlic, crushed

½ cup panko bread crumbs

¼ teaspoon salt

1 tablespoon toasted sesame seeds

Jalapeño peppers can sting and irritate the skin, so wear rubber gloves when handling peppers and do not touch your eyes.

1 Combine sauce ingredients in small bowl; set aside. Combine cucumber salad ingredients in medium bowl; set aside.

2 Preheat oven to 400°F. Line two baking sheets with parchment paper. Place quinoa in fine-mesh strainer; rinse well under cold running water. Combine quinoa and water in medium saucepan; heat to a boil. Reduce heat to low; cover and simmer 10 to 15 minutes or until quinoa is tender and water is absorbed. Cool slightly.

3 Combine remaining meatball ingredients, except sesame seeds in large bowl. Form 24 (2-inch) balls. Place on prepared baking sheets. Bake 10 minutes, brush with sauce; bake 3 minutes. Remove from oven; toss with remaining sauce.

4 Sprinkle meatballs with sesame seeds. Serve with cucumber salad.

Makes 6 servings

Tex-Mex Nachos

1 tablespoon vegetable oil

8 ounces ground beef

½ cup chopped onion

2 cloves garlic, minced

2 teaspoons chili powder

1 teaspoon ground cumin

½ teaspoon salt

½ teaspoon dried oregano

1 can (about 15 ounces) kidney beans, rinsed and drained

½ cup corn

½ cup sour cream, divided

2 tablespoons mayonnaise

1 tablespoon lime juice

¼ to ½ teaspoon chipotle chili powder

½ bag tortilla chips

½ (15-ounce) jar Cheddar cheese dip, warmed

½ cup pico de gallo

¼ cup guacamole

1 cup shredded iceberg lettuce

2 jalapeño peppers,* thinly sliced into rings

*Jalapeño peppers can sting and irritate the skin, so wear rubber gloves when handling peppers and do not touch your eyes.

1 Heat oil in large skillet over medium-high heat. Add beef, onion and garlic; cook and stir 6 minutes or until beef is no longer pink. Add chili powder, cumin, salt and oregano; cook and stir 1 minute. Add beans and corn; reduce heat to medium-low and cook 3 minutes or until heated through.

2 For chipotle sauce, combine ¼ cup sour cream, mayonnaise, lime juice and chipotle chili powder in small bowl; mix well. Place in small plastic squeeze bottle or small resealable food storage bag.

3 Spread tortilla chips on platter or large plate. Top with beef mixture; drizzle with cheese dip. Top with pico de gallo, guacamole, remaining ¼ cup sour cream, lettuce and jalapeño peppers. Drizzle chipotle sauce over nachos. Serve immediately.

Makes 4 to 6 servings

Breakfasts

Hawaiian Bread French Toast

6 eggs

1 cup milk

1 cup whipping cream

2 teaspoons coconut extract

2 teaspoons vanilla

1 teaspoon ground cinnamon

¼ cup sugar

1 pound sliced sweet Hawaiian bread or rolls, sliced

2 tablespoons unsalted butter, cut into ¼-inch pieces

½ cup coconut, toasted*

*To toast coconut, spread in single layer in heavy-bottomed skillet. Cook and stir over medium heat 1 to 2 minutes until lightly browned. Remove from skillet immediately. Cool before using.

Slow Cooker Directions

1 Coat inside of slow cooker with nonstick cooking spray. Whisk eggs, milk, cream and vanilla in large bowl. Combine cinnamon and sugar in small bowl.

2 Layer slices of bread in slow cooker, sprinkling with cinnamon-sugar mixture between layers. Pour egg mixture over top; press bread down with large spoon to absorb egg mixture. Dot with butter. Cover; cook on HIGH 2 hours. Sprinkle with toasted coconut.

Makes 8 to 10 servings

Scrambled Eggs with Smoked Salmon

1 container (16 ounces) cholesterol-free egg substitute

⅛ teaspoon black pepper

2 tablespoons sliced green onions, with tops

1 ounce cold reduced-fat cream cheese (Neufchâtel), cut into ¼-inch cubes

2 ounces smoked salmon, flaked

1 Whisk egg substitute and pepper in large bowl. Spray nonstick skillet with nonstick cooking spray; heat over medium heat. Pour egg substitute into skillet. Cook 5 to 7 minutes or until mixture begins to set, stirring occasionally while scraping bottom of pan.

2 Gently fold in green onions, cream cheese and salmon; cook and stir about 3 minutes or just until eggs are cooked through but still slightly moist.

Makes 4 servings

Blueberry Muffins

1 recipe Basic Muffin Mix, divided (recipe follows)

1½ cups fresh or frozen blueberries (do not thaw)

1 egg

¾ cup plus 2 tablespoons milk

½ cup (1 stick) butter, melted

1 teaspoon vanilla

½ teaspoon ground cinnamon

Dash ground nutmeg

1 Preheat oven to 400°F. Grease 15 standard (2½-inch) muffin cups or line with paper baking cups; set aside.

2 Prepare Basic Muffin Mix. Place ¼ cup Muffin Mix in small bowl. Add blueberries and toss to coat; set aside. (Do not thaw if using frozen blueberries.)

3 Beat egg in another small bowl; add milk, butter, vanilla cinnamon and nutmeg. Place remaining Muffin Mix in medium bowl. Add egg mixture and stir until almost blended; gently fold in blueberries. Fill prepared muffin cups three-fourths full.

4 Bake 20 to 25 minutes or until toothpick inserted into centers comes out clean. Cool in pan 2 minutes; remove muffins to wire rack. Serve warm or at room temperature.

Makes 15 muffins

Basic Muffin Mix

2 cups all-purpose flour

¾ cup sugar

2 teaspoons baking powder

½ teaspoon baking soda

¼ teaspoon salt

1 Combine all ingredients in medium bowl; stir until well blended.

2 Store Muffin Mix in airtight container or large resealable food storage bag at room temperature up to 12 months.

Chocolate-Cranberry Pumpkin Pancakes

2 cups all-purpose flour

⅓ cup packed brown sugar

2 teaspoons baking powder

½ teaspoon salt

½ teaspoon ground cinnamon

¼ teaspoon baking soda

¼ teaspoon ground ginger

¼ teaspoon ground nutmeg

1½ cups milk

2 eggs

½ cup solid-pack pumpkin

¼ cup vegetable oil

½ cup mini semisweet chocolate chips

½ cup dried cranberries

⅓ cup cinnamon chips

1 to 2 teaspoons butter, plus additional for serving

Maple syrup

1 Combine flour, brown sugar, baking powder, salt, cinnamon, baking soda, ginger and nutmeg in large bowl; mix well. Beat milk, eggs, pumpkin and oil in medium bowl until well blended. Add to flour mixture with chocolate chips, cranberries and cinnamon chips; stir just until dry ingredients are moistened.

2 Heat 1 teaspoon butter on griddle over medium heat. Pour batter by ¼ cupfuls onto griddle. Cook until bubbles form and bottom of pancakes are lightly browned; turn and cook 2 minutes or until browned and cooked through. Repeat with remaining batter, adding additional butter to griddle if necessary. Serve with maple syrup and additional butter, if desired.

Makes 16 to 18 pancakes

Spanish Potato Omelet

¼ cup olive oil

¼ cup vegetable oil

1 pound unpeeled red or white potatoes, cut into ⅛-inch slices

½ teaspoon salt, divided

1 small onion, cut in half lengthwise and thinly sliced crosswise

¼ cup chopped green bell pepper

¼ cup chopped red bell pepper

3 eggs

1 Heat oils in large skillet over medium-high heat. Add potatoes. Turn several times to coat slices with oil. Sprinkle with ¼ teaspoon salt. Cook 6 to 9 minutes or until potatoes are translucent, turning occasionally. Add onion and bell peppers. Reduce heat to medium. Cook 10 minutes or until potatoes are tender, turning occasionally. Drain mixture in colander placed in large bowl; reserve oil. Let potato mixture stand until cool. Beat eggs with remaining ¼ teaspoon salt in separate large bowl. Gently stir in potato mixture until covered with eggs. Let stand 15 minutes.

2 Heat 2 teaspoons reserved oil in small nonstick skillet over medium-high heat. Spread potato mixture in pan to form solid layer. Cook until egg mixture on bottom and side of pan is set but top still looks moist. Cover pan with plate. Flip omelet onto plate, then slide back into pan. Continue to cook until bottom is lightly browned. Slide omelet onto serving plate. Let stand 30 minutes before serving. Cut into wedges.

Makes 8 servings

German Apple Pancake

1 tablespoon butter

1 large *or* 2 small apples, peeled and thinly sliced (about 1½ cups)

1 tablespoon packed brown sugar

1½ teaspoons ground cinnamon, divided

2 eggs

2 egg whites

1 tablespoon granulated sugar

1 teaspoon vanilla

¼ teaspoon salt

½ cup all-purpose flour

½ cup milk

Maple syrup (optional)

1 Preheat oven to 425°F.

2 Melt butter in medium cast iron or ovenproof skillet* over medium heat. Add apples, brown sugar and ½ teaspoon cinnamon; cook and stir 5 minutes or until apples just begin to soften. Remove from heat. Arrange apple slices in single layer in skillet.

3 Whisk eggs, egg whites, granulated sugar, remaining 1 teaspoon cinnamon, vanilla and salt in medium bowl until well blended. Stir in flour and milk until smooth and well blended. Pour evenly over apples.

4 Bake 20 to 25 minutes or until puffed and golden brown. Serve with maple syrup, if desired.

To make skillet ovenproof, wrap handle in foil.

Makes 6 servings

Note: Pancake will fall slightly after being removed from the oven.

Three-Egg Omelet

3 eggs, lightly beaten

1 tablespoon water

Salt and black pepper

1 tablespoon butter or margarine

Fillings: shredded cheese, shredded crabmeat, cooked sliced mushrooms, cooked chopped onion, avocado slices, chopped ham, cooked small shrimp, cooked chopped bell pepper, chopped tomatoes, cooked chopped asparagus *and/ or* cooked chopped broccoli

1 Whisk eggs, water, salt and pepper in small bowl. Melt butter in 8-inch skillet over medium heat, tilting skillet to coat bottom of skillet. Pour egg mixture into skillet; cook without stirring until egg mixture begins to set. Gently lift cooked edge with spatula to allow uncooked eggs to flow underneath. Shake pan several times to loosen omelet. Cook until just set.

2 Place desired fillings on half of omelet. Carefully fold other half over fillings. Slide onto serving plate. Serve immediately.

Makes 1 serving

Chocolate Doughnuts

2¼ cups all-purpose flour, plus additional for work surface

½ cup unsweetened cocoa powder

¼ cup cornstarch

1 teaspoon salt

1 teaspoon baking powder

½ teaspoon baking soda

½ teaspoon ground cinnamon

½ teaspoon ground nutmeg

1 cup granulated sugar

2 eggs

¼ cup (½ stick) butter, melted

¼ cup applesauce

1 teaspoon vanilla

½ cup buttermilk

Vegetable oil for frying

Glaze

½ cup milk

1 cup semisweet or dark chocolate chips

½ teaspoon vanilla

1½ to 2 cups powdered sugar, sifted

Multicolored sprinkles

1 Whisk 2¼ cups flour, cocoa, cornstarch, salt, baking powder, baking soda, cinnamon and nutmeg in large bowl.

2 Beat 1 cup granulated sugar and eggs in large bowl with electric mixer on high speed 3 minutes or until pale and thick. Stir in butter, applesauce and 1 teaspoon vanilla. Add flour mixture alternately with buttermilk, mixing on low speed after each addition. Press plastic wrap directly onto surface of dough; refrigerate at least 1 hour.

3 Pour about 2 inches of oil into Dutch oven or large heavy saucepan; clip deep-fry or candy thermometer to side of pot. Heat over medium-high heat to 360° to 370°F.

4 Meanwhile, generously flour work surface. Turn out dough onto work surface and dust top with flour. Roll dough to about ¼-inch thickness; cut out doughnuts with floured doughnut cutter. Gather and reroll scraps. Line large wire rack with paper towels.

5 Working in batches, add doughnuts to hot oil. Cook 1 minute per side or until golden brown. Do not crowd the pan and adjust heat to maintain temperature during frying. Cool on wire racks.

6 For glaze, heat milk in small saucepan until bubbles form around edge of pan. Remove from heat. Add chocolate chips; let stand 1 minute to soften. Add ½ teaspoon vanilla; whisk until smooth. Whisk in enough powdered sugar to form stiff glaze. Dip tops of doughnuts in glaze; top with sprinkles. Let stand until glaze is set.

Makes 14 to 16 doughnuts

Maple Pecan Granola

¼ cup maple syrup

¼ cup packed dark brown sugar

1½ teaspoons vanilla

½ teaspoon ground cinnamon

½ teaspoon coarse salt

6 tablespoons vegetable oil

3 cups old-fashioned rolled oats

1½ cups pecans, coarsely chopped

¾ cup shredded coconut

¼ cup ground flaxseed

¼ cup water

Plain yogurt or milk (optional)

1 Preheat oven to 350°F. Line large rimmed baking sheet with parchment paper.

2 Whisk maple syrup, brown sugar, vanilla, cinnamon, salt and oil in large bowl until blended. Add oats, pecans, coconut and flaxseed; stir until evenly coated. Stir in water. Spread mixture on prepared baking sheet, pressing into even layer.

3 Bake 30 minutes or until granola is golden brown and fragrant. Cool completely on baking sheet. Serve with yogurt or milk, if desired. Store leftovers in an airtight container at room temperature 1 month.

Makes about 6 cups

Note: For chunky granola, do not stir during baking. For loose granola, stir every 10 minutes during baking.

Baked Apple Pancake

3 tablespoons butter

3 medium Granny Smith apples (about 1¼ pounds), peeled and cut into ¼-inch slices

½ cup packed dark brown sugar

1½ teaspoons ground cinnamon

½ teaspoon plus pinch salt, divided

4 eggs

⅓ cup whipping cream

⅓ cup milk

2 tablespoons granulated sugar

½ teaspoon vanilla

⅔ cup all-purpose flour

1 Melt butter in 8-inch ovenproof nonstick or cast iron skillet over medium heat. Add apples, brown sugar, cinnamon and pinch of salt; cook about 8 minutes or until apples begin to soften, stirring occasionally. Spread apples in even layer in skillet; set aside to cool 30 minutes.

2 After apples have cooled 30 minutes, preheat oven to 425°F. Whisk eggs in large bowl until foamy. Add whipping cream, milk, granulated sugar, vanilla and remaining ½ teaspoon salt; whisk until blended. Sift flour into egg mixture; whisk until batter is well blended and smooth. Set aside 15 minutes.

3 Stir batter; pour evenly over apple mixture. Place skillet on rimmed baking sheet in case of drips (or place baking sheet or piece of foil in oven beneath skillet).

4 Bake about 16 minutes or until top is golden brown and pancake is loose around edge. Cool 1 minute; loosen edge of pancake with spatula, if necessary. Place large serving plate or cutting board on top of skillet and invert pancake onto plate. Serve warm.

Makes 2 to 4 servings

Toasted Coconut Doughnuts

2¾ cups all-purpose flour, plus additional for work surface

¼ cup cornstarch

1½ teaspoons baking powder

1 teaspoon salt

½ teaspoon ground cinnamon

½ teaspoon ground nutmeg

1 cup granulated sugar

2 eggs

¼ cup (½ stick) butter, melted

¼ cup applesauce

1 teaspoon vanilla

¾ cup coconut milk, divided*

Vegetable oil for frying

1 cup flaked coconut

1 teaspoon dark rum or vanilla

1½ cups sifted powdered sugar

Shake the can vigorously to blend before opening the can.

1 Whisk 2¾ cup flour, cornstarch, baking powder, salt, cinnamon and nutmeg in large bowl.

2 Beat granulated sugar and eggs in large bowl with electric mixer on high speed 3 minutes or until pale and thick. Stir in butter, applesauce and vanilla. Add flour mixture alternately with ½ cup coconut milk, mixing on low speed after each addition. Press plastic wrap directly onto surface of dough; refrigerate at least 1 hour.

3 Pour about 2 inches of oil into Dutch oven or large heavy saucepan; clip deep-fry or candy thermometer to side of pot. Heat over medium-high heat to 360° to 370°F.

4 Meanwhile, generously flour work surface. Turn out dough onto work surface and dust top with flour. Roll dough about ¼ inch thick; cut out doughnuts with floured doughnut cutter. Gather and reroll scraps. Line large wire rack with paper towels.

5 Working in batches, add doughnuts to hot oil. Cook 1 minute per side or until golden brown. Do not crowd the pan and adjust heat to maintain temperature during frying. Cool on wire racks.

6 Spread coconut in large skillet; cook over medium-low heat about 10 minutes or until mostly golden brown, stirring frequently. Whisk remaining ¼ cup coconut milk and rum in medium bowl. Stir in powdered sugar to form smooth, thick glaze. Dip tops of doughnuts in glaze, letting excess drip back into bowl; immediately dip in coconut. Let stand until glaze is set.

Makes 14 to 16 doughnuts

Glazed Lemon Loaf

Cake

1½ cups all-purpose flour

½ teaspoon baking powder

½ teaspoon baking soda

½ teaspoon salt

1 cup granulated sugar

3 eggs

½ cup vegetable oil

⅓ cup lemon juice

2 tablespoons butter, melted

1 teaspoon lemon extract

½ teaspoon vanilla

Glaze

3 tablespoons butter

1½ cups powdered sugar

2 tablespoons lemon juice

1 to 2 teaspoons grated lemon peel

1 Preheat oven to 350°F. Grease and flour 8×4-inch loaf pan.

2 For cake, combine flour, baking powder, baking soda and salt in large bowl; mix well. Whisk granulated sugar, eggs, oil, ⅓ cup lemon juice, 2 tablespoons melted butter, lemon extract and vanilla in medium bowl until well blended. Add to flour mixture; stir just until blended. Pour batter into prepared pan.

3 Bake about 40 minutes or until toothpick inserted into center comes out clean. Cool in pan 10 minutes; remove to wire rack; cool 10 minutes.

4 Meanwhile, prepare glaze. Melt 3 tablespoons butter in small saucepan over medium-low heat. Whisk in powdered sugar, 2 tablespoons lemon juice and 1 teaspoon lemon peel; cook until smooth and hot, whisking constantly. Pour glaze over warm bread; smooth top. Cool completely before slicing. Garnish with additional 1 teaspoon lemon peel, if desired.

Makes 8 to 10 servings

Quick Jelly-Filled Biscuit Doughnuts

Vegetable oil for frying

1 can (about 7 ounces) refrigerated biscuit dough (10 biscuits)

⅓ cup coarse sugar

1 cup strawberry preserves*

*If preserves are very chunky, process in food processor 10 seconds or press through a fine-mesh sieve.

1 Pour about 2 inches of oil into Dutch oven or large heavy saucepan; clip deep-fry or candy thermometer to side of pot. Heat over medium-high heat to 360° to 370°F.

2 Separate biscuits. Place sugar in medium bowl. Fry biscuits in batches 1 minute per side until puffed and golden. Remove to wire rack. Immediately toss in sugar to coat.

3 Fit piping bag with medium star tip; fill bag with preserves. Poke hole in side of each doughnut with paring knife; fill with preserves. Serve immediately.

Makes 10 doughnuts

Soups

Chicken Noodle Soup

2 tablespoons butter

1 cup chopped onion

1 cup sliced carrots

½ cup diced celery

2 tablespoons vegetable oil

1 pound chicken breast tenderloins

1 pound chicken thigh fillets

4 cups chicken broth, divided

2 cups water

1 tablespoon minced fresh parsley, plus additional for garnish

1½ teaspoons salt

½ teaspoon black pepper

3 cups uncooked egg noodles

1 Melt butter in large saucepan or Dutch oven over medium-low heat. Add onion, carrots and celery; cook 15 minutes or until vegetables are soft, stirring occasionally.

2 Meanwhile, heat oil in large skillet over medium-high heat. Add chicken in single layer; cook about 12 minutes or until lightly browned and cooked through, turning once. Transfer chicken to cutting board. Add 1 cup broth to skillet; cook 1 minute, scraping up any browned bits from bottom of skillet. Add broth to vegetables. Stir in remaining 3 cups broth, water, 1 tablespoon parsley, salt and pepper.

3 Chop chicken into 1-inch pieces when cool enough to handle. Add to soup; bring to a boil over medium-high heat. Reduce heat to medium-low; cook 15 minutes. Add noodles; cook 15 minutes or until noodles are tender. Ladle into bowls; garnish with additional parsley.

Makes 8 servings

Creamy Tomato Soup

3 tablespoons olive oil, divided

2 tablespoons butter

1 large onion, finely chopped

2 cloves garlic, minced

2 teaspoons sugar

1 teaspoon salt

½ teaspoon dried oregano

2 cans (28 ounces each) peeled Italian plum tomatoes, undrained

4 cups ½-inch focaccia cubes (half of 9-ounce loaf)

½ teaspoon freshly ground black pepper

½ cup whipping cream

1 Heat 2 tablespoons oil and butter in large saucepan over medium-high heat. Add onion; cook and stir 5 minutes or until softened. Add garlic, sugar, salt and oregano; cook 30 seconds. Stir in tomatoes with juice; bring to a boil. Reduce heat to medium-low; simmer 45 minutes, stirring occasionally.

2 Meanwhile, prepare croutons. Preheat oven to 350°F. Combine focaccia cubes, remaining 1 tablespoon oil and pepper in large bowl; toss to coat. Spread on large rimmed baking sheet. Bake about 10 minutes or until bread cubes are golden brown.

3 Blend soup with immersion blender until smooth. (Or, process in batches in food processor or blender.) Stir in cream; heat through. Serve soup topped with croutons.

Makes 6 servings

Broccoli Cheese Soup

6 tablespoons (¾ stick) butter

1 cup chopped onion

1 clove garlic, minced

¼ cup all-purpose flour

2 cups vegetable broth

2 cups milk

1½ teaspoons Dijon mustard

½ teaspoon salt

¼ teaspoon ground nutmeg

¼ teaspoon black pepper

⅛ teaspoon hot pepper sauce

1 package (16 ounces) frozen broccoli

2 carrots, shredded (1 cup)

6 ounces pasteurized process cheese product, cubed

1 cup (4 ounces) shredded sharp Cheddar cheese, plus additional for garnish

1 Melt butter in large saucepan or Dutch oven over medium-low heat. Add onion; cook and stir 10 minutes or until softened. Add garlic; cook and stir 1 minute. Increase heat to medium. Whisk in flour until smooth; cook and stir 3 minutes without browning.

2 Gradually whisk in broth and milk. Add mustard, salt, nutmeg, black pepper and hot pepper sauce; cook 15 minutes or until thickened.

3 Add broccoli; cook 15 minutes. Add carrots; cook 10 minutes or until vegetables are tender.

4 Transfer half of soup to food processor or blender; process until smooth. Return to saucepan. Add cheese product and 1 cup Cheddar; cook and stir over low heat until cheese is melted. Ladle into bowls; garnish with additional Cheddar.

Makes 4 to 6 servings

Garden Vegetable Soup

1 tablespoon olive oil

1 medium onion, chopped

1 carrot, chopped

1 stalk celery, chopped

1 medium zucchini, diced

1 medium yellow squash, diced

1 red bell pepper, diced

2 tablespoons tomato paste

2 cloves garlic, minced

2 teaspoons salt

1 teaspoon Italian seasoning

½ teaspoon black pepper

8 cups vegetable broth

1 can (28 ounces) whole tomatoes, chopped, juice reserved

½ cup uncooked pearl barley

1 cup cut green beans (1-inch pieces)

½ cup corn

¼ cup slivered fresh basil

1 tablespoon lemon juice

1 Heat oil in large saucepan or Dutch oven over medium-high heat. Add onion, carrot and celery; cook and stir 8 minutes or until vegetables are softened. Add zucchini, yellow squash and bell pepper; cook and stir 5 minutes or until softened. Stir in tomato paste, garlic, salt, Italian seasoning and black pepper; cook 1 minute. Stir in broth and tomatoes with juice; bring to a boil. Stir in barley.

2 Reduce heat to low; cook 30 minutes. Stir in green beans and corn; cook about 15 minutes or until barley is tender and green beans are crisp-tender. Stir in basil and lemon juice.

Makes 8 to 10 servings

Shortcut Chicken Tortilla Soup

2 cans (about 14 ounces each) reduced-sodium chicken broth

4 boneless skinless chicken breasts (about 1 pound)

2 jars (16 ounces each) corn and black bean salsa

3 tablespoons vegetable oil

1 tablespoon taco seasoning mix

1 package (3 ounces) ramen noodles, any flavor, broken into small pieces*

1 cup (4 ounces) Monterey Jack cheese, grated

*Discard seasoning packet.

1 Bring broth to a simmer in large saucepan. Add chicken; cook 12 to 15 minutes or until no longer pink in center. Remove chicken to cutting board; set aside until cool enough to handle. Shred chicken with two forks.

2 Add salsa to saucepan; cook 5 minutes or until soup comes to a simmer. Return shredded chicken to saucepan; cook 5 minutes until thoroughly heated.

3 Combine oil and taco seasoning in small bowl. Add noodles; toss to coat. Cook and stir noodles in medium skillet over medium heat 8 to 10 minutes or until toasted. Top soup with toasted noodles and grated cheese.

Makes 6 servings

Tip: Serve soup with lime wedges, chopped avocado or fresh cilantro on the side—top with your favorites!

French Onion Soup

4 tablespoons (½ stick) butter

3 large yellow onions, sliced

1 cup dry white wine

3 cans (about 14 ounces each) beef or chicken broth

1 teaspoon Worcestershire sauce

½ teaspoon salt

½ teaspoon dried thyme

4 slices French bread, toasted

1 cup (4 ounces) shredded Swiss cheese

Fresh thyme (optional)

Slow Cooker Directions

1 Melt butter in large skillet over medium heat. Add onions, cook and stir 15 minutes or until onions are soft and lightly browned. Stir in wine.

2 Combine onion mixture, broth, Worcestershire sauce, salt and dried thyme in slow cooker. Cover; cook on LOW 4 to 4½ hours.

3 Ladle soup into four bowls; top with bread slice and cheese. Broil 4 inches from heat 2 to 3 minutes or until cheese is bubbly and browned. Garnish with fresh thyme.

Makes 4 servings

Chili

1½ pounds ground beef

1½ cups chopped onion

1 cup chopped green bell pepper

2 cloves garlic, minced

3 cans (about 15 ounces each) dark red kidney beans, rinsed and drained

2 cans (about 15 ounces each) tomato sauce

1 can (about 14 ounces) diced tomatoes

2 to 3 teaspoons chili powder

1 to 2 teaspoons dry hot mustard

¾ teaspoon dried basil

½ teaspoon black pepper

1 to 2 dried hot chile peppers (optional)

Shredded Cheddar cheese (optional)

Fresh cilantro leaves (optional)

Slow Cooker Directions

1 Cook and stir beef, onion, bell pepper and garlic in large skillet over medium-high heat 6 to 8 minutes or until beef is browned and onion is tender. Drain fat. Transfer to slow cooker.

2 Add beans, tomato sauce, diced tomatoes, chili powder, dry mustard, basil, black pepper and chile peppers, if desired, to slow cooker; mix well. Cover; cook on LOW 8 to 10 hours or on HIGH 4 to 5 hours. Remove and discard chiles before serving. Top with cheese, if desired. Garnish with cilantro.

Makes 6 servings

Chicken Enchilada Soup

2 tablespoons vegetable oil, divided

1½ pounds boneless skinless chicken breasts, cut into ½-inch cubes

½ cup chopped onion

2 cloves garlic, minced

2 cans (about 14 ounces each) chicken broth

3 cups water, divided

1 cup masa harina

1 package (16 ounces) pasteurized process cheese product, cubed

1 can (10 ounces) mild red enchilada sauce

1 teaspoon chili powder

½ teaspoon salt

½ teaspoon ground cumin

Chopped fresh tomatoes

Crispy tortilla strips*

*If tortilla strips are not available, crumble tortilla chips into bite-size pieces.

1 Heat 1 tablespoon oil in large saucepan or Dutch oven over medium-high heat. Add chicken; cook and stir 10 minutes or until no longer pink. Transfer chicken to large bowl with slotted spoon; drain fat from saucepan.

2 Heat remaining 1 tablespoon oil in same saucepan over medium-high heat. Add onion and garlic; cook and stir 3 minutes or until softened. Stir in broth.

3 Whisk 2 cups water into masa harina in large bowl until smooth. Whisk mixture into broth in saucepan. Stir in cheese product, remaining 1 cup water, enchilada sauce, chili powder, salt and cumin; bring to a boil over high heat. Add chicken. Reduce heat to medium-low; cook 30 minutes, stirring frequently. Ladle soup into bowls; top with tomatoes and tortilla strips.

Makes 8 to 10 servings

Minestrone Soup

1 tablespoon olive oil

½ cup chopped onion

1 stalk celery, diced

1 carrot, diced

2 cloves garlic, minced

2 cups vegetable broth

1½ cups water

1 bay leaf

¾ teaspoon salt

½ teaspoon dried basil

½ teaspoon dried oregano

¼ teaspoon dried thyme

¼ teaspoon sugar

⅛ teaspoon ground black pepper

1 can (about 15 ounces) dark red kidney beans, rinsed and drained

1 can (about 15 ounces) navy beans or cannellini beans, rinsed and drained

1 can (about 14 ounces) diced tomatoes

1 cup diced zucchini (about 1 small)

½ cup uncooked small shell pasta

½ cup frozen cut green beans

¼ cup dry red wine

1 cup packed chopped fresh spinach

Grated Parmesan cheese (optional)

1 Heat oil in large saucepan or Dutch oven over medium-high heat. Add onion, celery, carrot and garlic; cook and stir 5 to 7 minutes or until vegetables are tender. Add broth, water, bay leaf, salt, basil, oregano, thyme, sugar and pepper; bring to a boil.

2 Stir in kidney beans, navy beans, tomatoes, zucchini, pasta, green beans and wine; cook 10 minutes, stirring occasionally.

3 Add spinach; cook 2 minutes or until pasta and zucchini are tender. Remove and discard bay leaf. Ladle into bowls; garnish with cheese.

Makes 4 to 6 servings

Italian Wedding Soup

2 eggs

6 cloves garlic, minced, divided

2 teaspoons salt, divided

⅛ teaspoon black pepper

1½ pounds meat loaf mix (ground beef and pork)

¾ cup plain dry bread crumbs

½ cup grated Parmesan cheese

2 tablespoons olive oil

1 onion, chopped

2 carrots, chopped

2 heads escarole or curly endive, coarsely chopped

8 cups chicken broth

1 can (about 14 ounces) Italian plum tomatoes, coarsely chopped, juice reserved

3 sprigs fresh thyme

½ teaspoon red pepper flakes

1 cup uncooked acini di pepe pasta

1 Whisk eggs, 2 cloves garlic, 1 teaspoon salt and black pepper in large bowl until blended. Stir in meat loaf mix, bread crumbs and cheese; mix gently until well blended. Shape mixture by tablespoonfuls into 1-inch balls.

2 Heat oil in large saucepan or Dutch oven over medium heat. Cook meatballs in batches about 5 minutes or until browned. Remove to plate; set aside.

3 Add onion, carrots and remaining 4 cloves garlic to saucepan; cook and stir about 5 minutes or until onion is lightly browned. Add escarole; cook 2 minutes or until wilted. Stir in broth, tomatoes, thyme, remaining 1 teaspoon salt and red pepper flakes; bring to a boil over high heat. Reduce heat to medium-low; cook 15 minutes.

4 Add meatballs and pasta to soup; return to a boil over high heat. Reduce heat to medium; cook 10 minutes or until pasta is tender. Remove thyme sprigs before serving.

Makes 8 servings

Lentil Soup

2 tablespoons olive oil, divided

2 medium onions, chopped

1½ teaspoons salt

4 cloves garlic, minced

¼ cup tomato paste

1 teaspoon dried oregano

½ teaspoon dried basil

¼ teaspoon dried thyme

¼ teaspoon black pepper

½ cup dry sherry or white wine

8 cups vegetable broth

2 cups water

3 carrots, cut into ½-inch pieces

2 cups dried lentils, rinsed and sorted

1 cup chopped fresh parsley

1 tablespoon balsamic vinegar

1 Heat 1 tablespoon oil in large saucepan or Dutch oven over medium heat. Add onions; cook 10 minutes, stirring occasionally. Add remaining 1 tablespoon oil and salt; cook 10 minutes or until onions are golden brown, stirring frequently.

2 Add garlic; cook and stir 1 minute. Add tomato paste, oregano, basil, thyme and pepper; cook and stir 1 minute. Stir in sherry; cook 30 seconds, scraping up browned bits from bottom of saucepan.

3 Stir in broth, water, carrots and lentils; cover and bring to a boil over high heat. Reduce heat to medium-low; cook, partially covered, 30 minutes or until lentils are tender.

4 Remove from heat; stir in parsley and vinegar.

Makes 6 to 8 servings

Beef Vegetable Soup

1½ pounds cubed beef
   stew meat

¼ cup all-purpose flour

3 tablespoons vegetable
   oil, divided

1 onion, chopped

2 stalks celery, chopped

3 tablespoons tomato
   paste

2 teaspoons salt

1 teaspoon dried thyme

½ teaspoon garlic powder

¼ teaspoon black pepper

6 cups beef broth, divided

1 can (28 ounces) stewed
   tomatoes, undrained

1 tablespoon
   Worcestershire sauce

1 bay leaf

4 unpeeled red potatoes
   (about 1 pound), cut
   into 1-inch pieces

3 medium carrots, cut in
   half lengthwise then
   cut into ½-inch slices

6 ounces green beans,
   trimmed and cut into
   1-inch pieces

1 cup frozen corn

1 Combine beef and flour in medium bowl; toss to coat. Heat 1 tablespoon oil in large saucepan or Dutch oven over medium-high heat. Cook beef in two batches about 5 minutes or until browned on all sides, adding additional 1 tablespoon oil after first batch. Transfer beef to medium bowl.

2 Heat remaining 1 tablespoon oil in same saucepan. Add onion and celery; cook and stir about 5 minutes or until softened. Add tomato paste, 2 teaspoons salt, thyme, garlic powder and ¼ teaspoon pepper; cook and stir 1 minute. Stir in 1 cup broth, scraping up browned bits from bottom of saucepan. Stir in remaining 5 cups broth, tomatoes, Worcestershire sauce, bay leaf and beef; bring to a boil.

3 Reduce heat to low; cover and cook 1 hour and 20 minutes. Add potatoes and carrots; cook 15 minutes. Add green beans and corn; cook 15 minutes or until vegetables are tender. Remove and discard bay leaf. Season with additional salt and pepper.

Makes 6 to 8 servings

Mexican Tortilla Soup

- 6 to 8 (6-inch) corn tortillas, preferably day-old
- 2 large very ripe tomatoes (about 1 pound), peeled, seeded and cut into chunks
- ⅔ cup coarsely chopped white onion
- 1 clove garlic
- Vegetable oil
- 7 cups chicken broth
- 4 sprigs fresh cilantro
- 3 sprigs fresh mint (optional)
- ½ to 1 teaspoon salt
- 4 or 5 dried pasilla chiles
- 5 ounces queso Chihuahua or Monterey Jack cheese, cut into ½-inch cubes
- ¼ cup coarsely chopped fresh cilantro

1 Stack tortillas; cut stack into ½-inch-wide strips. Let tortilla strips stand, uncovered, on wire rack 1 to 2 hours to dry slightly.

2 Combine tomatoes, onion and garlic in blender or food processor; blend until smooth. Heat 3 tablespoons oil in large saucepan over medium heat until hot. Add tomato mixture; cook 10 minutes, stirring frequently. Add broth and cilantro sprigs; bring to a boil over high heat. Reduce heat to low; simmer, uncovered, 20 minutes. Add mint, if desired, and salt; simmer 10 minutes. Remove and discard cilantro and mint sprigs. Keep soup warm.

3 Heat ½ inch oil in large deep skillet over medium-high heat to 375°F; adjust heat to maintain temperature. Fry half of tortilla strips at a time, in single layer, 1 minute or until crisp, turning occasionally. Remove with slotted spoon; drain on paper towel-lined plate.

4 Fry chiles in same oil about 30 seconds or until puffed and crisp, turning occasionally. *Do not burn chiles.* Drain on paper towel-lined plate. Cool slightly; crumble into coarse pieces.

5 Ladle soup into bowls; serve with chiles, tortilla strips, cheese and chopped cilantro.

Makes 4 to 6 servings

Main Dishes

Pot Roast

1 tablespoon vegetable oil

1 boneless beef chuck shoulder roast (3 to 4 pounds)

6 medium potatoes, halved

6 carrots, cut into chunks

2 onions, quartered

2 stalks celery, sliced

1 can (about 14 ounces) diced tomatoes, undrained

Salt and black pepper

Dried oregano

Water

1½ to 2 tablespoons all-purpose flour

Slow Cooker Directions

1 Heat oil in large skillet over medium-low heat. Add roast; brown on all sides. Transfer to slow cooker.

2 Add potatoes, carrots, onions, celery and tomatoes with juice. Season with salt, pepper and oregano. Add enough water to cover bottom of slow cooker by about ½ inch. Cover; cook on LOW 8 to 10 hours. Remove roast to platter. Let stand 15 minutes.

3 Transfer juices to small saucepan. Whisk in flour until smooth. Cook and stir over medium heat until thickened. Slice roast and serve with gravy and vegetables.

Makes 6 to 8 servings

Spicy Buttermilk Oven-Fried Chicken

1 cut-up whole chicken (about 3½ pounds)

2 cups buttermilk

1½ cups all-purpose flour

1 teaspoon salt

1 teaspoon ground red pepper

½ teaspoon garlic powder

¼ cup canola oil

1 Place chicken pieces in single layer in 13×9-inch baking dish. Pour buttermilk over chicken. Cover with plastic wrap and refrigerate; let marinate at least 2 hours.

2 Preheat oven to 350°F. Combine flour, salt, red pepper and garlic powder in large shallow bowl. Heat oil in large skillet over medium-high heat until hot.

3 Remove chicken pieces from buttermilk; coat with flour mixture. Place chicken in hot oil; cook about 10 minutes or until brown and crisp on all sides. Place chicken in single layer in 13×9-inch baking dish. Bake, uncovered, 30 to 45 minutes or until chicken is cooked through (165°F).

Makes 6 servings

Turkey Meat Loaf

1 pound ground white meat turkey

1 pound ground dark meat turkey

1 medium onion, chopped

½ cup seasoned dry bread crumbs

⅓ cup plus ¼ cup ketchup, divided

2 tablespoons yellow mustard

1 egg

1 teaspoon garlic powder

1 teaspoon dried oregano

1 teaspoon dried basil

1 teaspoon Worcestershire sauce

½ teaspoon salt

¼ teaspoon black pepper

Slow Cooker Directions

1 Coat inside of slow cooker with nonstick cooking spray. Prepare foil handles by tearing off four 18×2-inch strips heavy foil (or use regular foil folded to double thickness). Crisscross foil strips in spoke design; place in slow cooker. Spray foil handles with nonstick cooking spray.

2 Combine ground turkey, onion, bread crumbs, ¼ cup ketchup, mustard, egg, garlic powder, oregano, basil, Worcestershire sauce, salt and pepper in large bowl; mix well. Form mixture into 9×4-inch loaf. Place loaf on top of foil. Spread top of meat loaf with remaining ⅓ cup ketchup. Cover; cook on HIGH 3½ to 4 hours or on LOW 7 to 8 hours. Remove meat loaf from slow cooker using foil handles to large cutting board. Let stand 10 minutes before slicing.

Makes 6 to 8 servings

Spicy Chicken Rigatoni

2 tablespoons olive oil

2 cloves garlic, minced

½ teaspoon red pepper flakes

½ teaspoon black pepper

8 ounces boneless skinless chicken breasts, cut into thin strips

1 cup marinara sauce

¾ cup prepared Alfredo sauce

1 package (16 ounces) mezzo rigatoni, rigatoni or penne pasta, cooked until al dente

¾ cup frozen peas, thawed

Grated Parmesan cheese (optional)

1 Heat oil in large saucepan over medium-high heat. Add garlic, red pepper flakes and black pepper; cook and stir 1 minute. Add chicken; cook and stir 4 minutes or until cooked through.

2 Add marinara sauce and Alfredo sauce; stir until blended. Reduce heat to medium-low; cook 10 minutes, stirring occasionally.

3 Add pasta and peas; stir gently to coat. Cook 2 minutes or until heated through. Sprinkle with cheese, if desired.

Makes 4 servings

Patty Melts

5 tablespoons butter, divided

2 large yellow onions, thinly sliced

¾ teaspoon plus pinch salt, divided

1 pound ground chuck (80% lean)

½ teaspoon garlic powder

½ teaspoon onion powder

¼ teaspoon black pepper

8 slices marble rye bread

½ cup Thousand Island dressing

8 slices deli American or Swiss cheese

1 Melt 2 tablespoons butter in large skillet over medium heat. Add onions and pinch of salt; cook 20 minutes or until onions are very soft and golden brown, stirring occasionally. Remove to small bowl; wipe out skillet with paper towel.

2 Combine beef, remaining ¾ teaspoon salt, garlic powder, onion powder and pepper in medium bowl; mix gently. Shape into four patties about the size and shape of bread slices and ¼ to ½ inch thick.

3 Melt 1 tablespoon butter in same skillet over medium-high heat. Add patties, two at a time; cook 3 minutes or until bottoms are browned, pressing down gently to form crust. Turn patties; cook 3 minutes or until browned. Remove patties to plate; wipe out skillet with paper towel.

4 Spread one side of each bread slice with dressing. Top four bread slices with cheese slice, patty, caramelized onions, another cheese slice and remaining bread slices.

5 Melt 1 tablespoon butter in same skillet over medium heat. Add two sandwiches to skillet; cook 4 minutes or until golden brown, pressing down to crisp bread. Turn sandwiches; cook 4 minutes or until golden brown and cheese is melted. Repeat with remaining 1 tablespoon butter and remaining sandwiches.

Makes 4 servings

Vegetable Penne Italiano

1 tablespoon olive oil

1 red bell pepper, cut into ½-inch pieces

1 green bell pepper, cut into ½-inch pieces

1 medium sweet onion, halved and thinly sliced

3 cloves garlic, minced

2 tablespoons tomato paste

2 teaspoons salt

1 teaspoon sugar

1 teaspoon Italian seasoning

¼ teaspoon black pepper

1 can (28 ounces) Italian plum tomatoes, chopped, juice reserved

8 ounces uncooked penne pasta

Grated Parmesan cheese

Chopped fresh basil

1 Heat oil in large skillet over medium-high heat. Add bell peppers, onion and garlic; cook and stir 8 minutes or until vegetables are crisp-tender.

2 Add tomato paste, salt, sugar, Italian seasoning and black pepper; cook and stir 1 minute. Stir in tomatoes with juice. Reduce heat to medium-low; cook 15 minutes or until vegetables are tender and sauce is thickened.

3 Meanwhile, cook pasta in large saucepan of salted water according to package directions for al dente. Drain pasta; return to saucepan. Add sauce; stir gently to coat. Divide among four serving bowls; top with cheese and basil.

Makes 4 servings

Fish & Chips

¾ cup all-purpose flour

½ cup flat beer or lemon-lime carbonated beverage

Vegetable oil

4 medium russet potatoes, each cut into 8 wedges

Salt

1 egg, separated

1 pound cod fillets (about 6 to 8 small fillets)

Malt vinegar (optional)

Lemon wedges (optional)

1 Combine flour, beer and 2 teaspoons oil in small bowl. Cover and refrigerate 1 to 2 hours.

2 Pour 2 inches oil into large heavy skillet; heat to 365°F over medium heat. Add potato wedges in batches. *Do not crowd.* Fry 4 to 6 minutes or until browned, turning once. *Allow temperature of oil to return to 365°F between batches.* Drain on paper towels; sprinkle lightly with salt. Reserve oil to fry cod.

3 Stir egg yolk into flour mixture. Beat egg white in medium bowl with electric mixer at medium-high speed until soft peaks form. Fold egg white into flour mixture.

4 Return oil to 365°F. Dip fish pieces into batter in batches; fry 4 to 6 minutes or until batter is crispy and brown and fish begins to flake when tested with fork, turning once. *Allow temperature of oil to return to 365°F between batches.* Drain on paper towels. Serve immediately with potato wedges. Sprinkle with vinegar and serve with lemon wedges, if desired.

Makes 4 servings

Southern Buttermilk Fried Chicken

2 cups all-purpose flour

1½ teaspoons celery salt

1 teaspoon dried thyme

¾ teaspoon black pepper

½ teaspoon dried marjoram

1¾ cups buttermilk

2 cups vegetable oil

3 pounds chicken pieces

1 Combine flour, celery salt, thyme, pepper and marjoram in shallow bowl. Pour buttermilk into medium bowl.

2 Heat oil in heavy deep skillet over medium heat until 350°F on deep-fry thermometer.

3 Dip chicken into buttermilk, one piece at a time; shake off excess. Coat with flour mixture; shake off excess. Dip again in buttermilk and coat once more with flour mixture. Fry chicken in batches, skin side down, 10 to 12 minutes or until browned. Turn and fry 12 to 14 minutes or until cooked through (165°F). *Allow temperature of oil to return to 350°F between batches.* Drain chicken on paper towels.

Makes 4 servings

Note: Carefully monitor the temperature of the vegetable oil during cooking. It should not drop below 325°F or go higher than 350°F. The chicken can also be cooked in a deep fryer following the manufacturer's directions. Never leave hot oil unattended.

Old-Fashioned Meat Loaf

1 teaspoon olive oil

1 cup finely chopped
  onion

4 cloves garlic, minced

1½ pounds extra-lean
  ground beef

1 cup chili sauce, divided

¾ cup old-fashioned oats

2 egg whites

½ teaspoon black pepper

¼ teaspoon salt (optional)

1 tablespoon Dijon
  mustard

1 Preheat oven to 375°F. Heat oil in large nonstick skillet over medium heat. Add onion; cook and stir 5 minutes. Add garlic; cook and stir 1 minute. Transfer to large bowl; cool 5 minutes.

2 Add beef, ½ cup chili sauce, oats, egg whites, pepper and salt, if desired, to bowl; mix well. Pat into 9×5-inch loaf pan. Combine remaining ½ cup chili sauce and mustard in small bowl; spoon evenly over top of meat loaf.

3 Bake 45 to 50 minutes or until cooked through (165°F). Let stand 5 minutes. Pour off any juices from pan. Cut into slices.

Makes 6 servings

Almond Chicken Salad Sandwich

¼ cup mayonnaise

¼ cup plain Greek yogurt
or sour cream

2 tablespoons cider
vinegar

1 tablespoon honey

1 teaspoon salt

½ teaspoon black pepper

⅛ teaspoon garlic powder

2 cups chopped cooked
chicken

¾ cup halved red grapes

1 large stalk celery,
chopped

⅓ cup sliced almonds

Leaf lettuce

1 tomato, thinly sliced

8 slices sesame semolina
or country Italian
bread

1 Whisk mayonnaise, yogurt, vinegar, honey, salt, pepper and garlic powder in small bowl until well blended.

2 Combine chicken, grapes and celery in medium bowl. Add dressing; toss gently to coat. Cover and refrigerate several hours or overnight. Stir in almonds just before making sandwiches.

3 Place lettuce and tomato slices on four bread slices; top with chicken salad and remaining bread slices. Serve immediately.

Makes 4 servings

Lasagna

6 uncooked whole wheat lasagna noodles

½ pound extra-lean ground beef

1 cup chopped onion

2 cloves garlic, minced

1 jar (26 ounces) tomato-basil pasta sauce

1 container (15 ounces) fat-free cottage cheese

2 egg whites

¼ cup chopped fresh basil, divided

2 cups (8 ounces) shredded part-skim mozzarella cheese, divided

1 Preheat oven to 375°F.

2 Cook noodles according to package directions, omitting salt and fat; drain. Rinse with cold water; drain again. Set aside.

3 Brown beef, onion and garlic in large saucepan over medium-high heat 6 to 8 minutes, stirring to break up meat. Drain fat. Add pasta sauce; bring to a boil. Reduce heat; simmer 5 minutes.

4 Stir cottage cheese, egg whites and 2 tablespoons basil in medium bowl until just combined. Spoon 1 cup sauce mixture over bottom of 13×9-inch baking dish. Layer three noodles over sauce mixture. Spoon cottage cheese mixture over noodles. Top with half of remaining sauce mixture and 1 cup mozzarella cheese. Top with remaining three noodles and pasta sauce mixture.

5 Cover with foil. Bake 30 minutes or until heated through.

6 Remove foil; sprinkle with remaining 1 cup mozzarella cheese and 2 tablespoons basil. Bake 5 minutes or until cheese is melted. Let stand 5 minutes before serving.

Makes 8 servings

Note: Leftovers reheat well in microwave.

Chicken Marsala

4 boneless skinless chicken breasts (6 to 8 ounces each)

½ cup all-purpose flour

1 teaspoon coarse salt

¼ teaspoon black pepper

2 tablespoons olive oil

3 tablespoons butter, divided

2 cups (16 ounces) sliced mushrooms

1 shallot, minced (about 2 tablespoons)

1 clove garlic, minced

1 cup dry Marsala wine

½ cup chicken broth

Finely chopped fresh parsley

1 Pound chicken to ¼-inch thickness between two sheets plastic wrap. Combine flour, salt and pepper in shallow dish; mix well. Coat both sides of chicken with flour mixture, shaking off excess.

2 Heat oil and 1 tablespoon butter in large skillet over medium-high heat. Add chicken in single layer; cook about 4 minutes per side or until golden brown. Remove to plate; cover loosely with foil to keep warm.

3 Add 1 tablespoon butter, mushrooms and shallot to skillet; cook about 10 minutes or until mushrooms are deep golden brown, stirring occasionally. Add garlic; cook and stir 1 minute. Stir in wine and broth; cook 2 minutes, scraping up browned bits from bottom of skillet. Stir in remaining 1 tablespoon butter until melted.

4 Return chicken to skillet; turn to coat with sauce. Cook 2 minutes or until heated through. Sprinkle with parsley.

Makes 4 servings

Breaded Veal Scallopini with Exotic Mushrooms

½ pound veal cutlets

½ teaspoon salt, divided

¼ teaspoon black pepper, divided

1 egg

1 tablespoon milk or water

½ cup dry bread crumbs

5 tablespoons unsalted butter, divided

2 tablespoons olive oil, divided

2 large shallots, chopped (about ¼ cup)

8 ounces exotic mushrooms, such as cremini, oyster, baby bella and shiitake*

½ teaspoon herbes de Provence**

½ cup reduced-sodium chicken broth

2 lemon wedges (optional)

*Exotic mushrooms make this dish special. However, you can substitute white button mushrooms, if you prefer.

**Herbes de Provence is a mixture of basil, fennel, lavender, marjoram, rosemary, sage, savory and thyme used to season meat, poultry and vegetables.

1 Season cutlets with ¼ teaspoon salt and ⅛ teaspoon pepper. Lightly beat egg with milk in shallow dish. Place bread crumbs in separate shallow dish.

2 Dip cutlet into egg, letting excess drip off. Dip in bread crumbs, turning to coat. Repeat with remaining cutlets.

3 Heat 1 tablespoon butter and 1 tablespoon oil in large nonstick skillet over medium-high heat. Cook half of cutlets 3 minutes or until golden brown and cooked through, turning once. Transfer to plate. Add 1 tablespoon butter and remaining 1 tablespoon oil; repeat with remaining cutlets.

4 Wipe out skillet with paper towel. Melt remaining 3 tablespoons butter over medium-high heat. Add shallots; cook and stir 1 to 2 minutes or until translucent. Add mushrooms, remaining ¼ teaspoon salt, ⅛ teaspoon pepper and herbes de Provence; cook and stir 3 to 4 minutes or until most of liquid is evaporated. Stir in broth; cook 2 to 3 minutes or until slightly thickened.

5 Pour mushroom mixture over cutlets. Garnish with lemon wedges.

Makes 2 servings

Fettuccine Alfredo

12 ounces uncooked fettuccine

⅔ cup whipping cream

6 tablespoons (¾ stick) butter

½ teaspoon salt

Generous dash white pepper

Generous dash ground nutmeg

1 cup grated Parmesan cheese

2 tablespoons chopped fresh Italian parsley

1 Cook pasta according to package directions. Drain well; cover and keep warm in saucepan.

2 Meanwhile, heat cream and butter in large heavy skillet over medium-low heat until butter melts and mixture bubbles, stirring frequently. Cook and stir 2 minutes. Stir in salt, pepper and nutmeg. Remove from heat; gradually stir in Parmesan until well blended and smooth. Return to low heat, if necessary; do not let sauce bubble or cheese will become lumpy and tough.

3 Pour sauce over pasta. Cook and stir over low heat 2 to 3 minutes or until sauce is thickened and pasta is evenly coated. Sprinkle with parsley. Serve immediately.

Makes 4 servings

Spicy Beef Tacos

1 pound boneless beef chuck, cut into 1-inch cubes

Vegetable oil

1 to 2 teaspoons chili powder

1 clove garlic, minced

½ teaspoon salt

½ teaspoon ground cumin

1 can (about 14 ounces) diced tomatoes, undrained

12 (6-inch) corn tortillas*

1 cup (4 ounces) shredded mild Cheddar cheese

2 to 3 cups shredded iceberg lettuce

1 large fresh tomato, seeded and chopped

Chopped fresh cilantro (optional)

Or, substitute packaged taco shells for the corn tortillas. Omit steps 4 and 5. Warm taco shells according to package directions.

1 Brown beef in 2 tablespoons hot oil in large skillet over medium-high heat 10 to 12 minutes, turning frequently. Reduce heat to low. Stir in chili powder, garlic, salt and cumin. Cook and stir 30 seconds.

2 Add diced tomatoes with juice. Bring to a boil over high heat. Reduce heat to low. Cover and simmer 1½ to 2 hours or until beef is very tender.

3 Using two forks, pull beef into coarse shreds in skillet. Increase heat to medium. Cook, uncovered, 10 to 15 minutes or until most of liquid has evaporated. Keep warm.

4 Heat 4 to 5 inches oil in deep fat fryer or deep saucepan over medium-high heat to 375°F; adjust heat to maintain temperature.

5 For taco shells, place 1 tortilla in taco fryer basket;** close gently. Fry tortilla 30 seconds to 1 minute until crisp and golden. Open basket; gently remove taco shell. Drain on paper towel-lined plate. Repeat with remaining tortillas.

6 Fill taco shells with beef, cheese, lettuce and chopped tomato. Garnish with cilantro, if desired.

***Taco fryer baskets are available in large supermarkets and in houseware stores.*

Makes 6 servings

Chicken Piccata

3 tablespoons all-purpose flour

½ teaspoon salt

¼ teaspoon black pepper

4 boneless skinless chicken breasts (4 ounces each)

2 teaspoons olive oil

1 teaspoon butter

2 cloves garlic, minced

¾ cup chicken broth

1 tablespoon fresh lemon juice

2 tablespoons chopped fresh Italian parsley

1 tablespoon capers, drained

1 Combine flour, salt and pepper in shallow dish. Reserve 1 tablespoon flour mixture.

2 Pound chicken between waxed paper to ½-inch thickness with flat side of meat mallet or rolling pin. Coat chicken with remaining flour mixture, shaking off excess.

3 Heat oil and butter in large nonstick skillet over medium heat. Add chicken; cook 4 to 5 minutes per side or until no longer pink in center. Transfer to serving platter; cover loosely with foil.

4 Add garlic to same skillet; cook and stir 1 minute. Add reserved flour mixture; cook and stir 1 minute. Add broth and lemon juice; cook 2 minutes or until thickened, stirring frequently. Stir in parsley and capers; spoon sauce over chicken.

Makes 4 servings

Tuna Noodle Casserole

7 ounces (2 cups)
  uncooked elbow
  macaroni

2 tablespoons butter

¾ cup chopped onion
  (½ large onion)

½ cup thinly sliced celery
  (2 stalks)

½ cup finely chopped red
  bell pepper

2 tablespoons
  all-purpose flour

½ teaspoon salt

⅛ teaspoon white pepper

1½ cups milk

1 can (6 ounces) albacore
  tuna in water, drained

½ cup grated Parmesan
  cheese, divided

1 Preheat oven to 375°F. Spray 8-inch square baking dish with nonstick cooking spray.

2 Cook pasta according to package directions until al dente. Drain and set aside.

3 Meanwhile, melt butter in large deep skillet over medium heat. Add onion; cook and stir 3 minutes. Add celery and bell pepper; cook and stir 3 minutes. Add flour, salt and pepper to vegetables; cook and stir 1 minute. Gradually stir in milk; bring to a boil. Cook and stir 2 minutes or until thickened. Remove from heat.

4 Add pasta, tuna and ¼ cup cheese to skillet; stir until pasta is well coated. Pour tuna mixture into prepared dish; sprinkle evenly with remaining ¼ cup cheese.

5 Bake, uncovered, 20 to 25 minutes or until hot and bubbly.

Makes 4 servings

Spaghetti & Meatballs

6 ounces uncooked multigrain or whole wheat spaghetti

¾ pound extra lean ground beef

¼ pound hot turkey Italian sausage, casing removed

1 egg white

2 tablespoons plain dry bread crumbs

1 teaspoon dried oregano

2 cups tomato-basil pasta sauce

3 tablespoons chopped fresh basil

2 tablespoons grated Parmesan cheese

1 Preheat oven to 450°F. Spray baking sheet with nonstick cooking spray. Cook spaghetti acording to package directions, omiting salt and fat. Drain and keep warm.

2 Combine beef, sausage, egg white, bread crumbs and oregano in medium bowl; mix well. Shape mixture into 16 (1½-inch) meatballs. Place on prepared baking sheet; coat with cooking spray. Bake 12 minutes, turning once.

3 Pour pasta sauce into large skillet. Add meatballs; cook over medium heat 9 minutes or until sauce is heated through and meatballs are cooked through (160°F), stirring occasionally. Divide spaghetti among four places. Top with meatballs and sauce; sprinkle with basil and cheese.

Makes 4 servings

Pesto with Linguine

12 ounces uncooked linguine

2 tablespoons butter

¼ cup plus 1 tablespoon olive oil, divided

2 tablespoons pine nuts

1 cup tightly packed fresh basil leaves

2 cloves garlic

¼ teaspoon salt

¼ cup grated Parmesan cheese

1½ tablespoons grated Romano cheese

1 Cook linguine according to package directions; drain. Toss with butter in large serving bowl; set aside and keep warm.

2 Meanwhile, heat 1 tablespoon oil in small skillet over medium-low heat. Add pine nuts; cook and stir 30 to 45 seconds until light brown, shaking pan constantly. Remove with slotted spoon; drain on paper towel-lined plate.

3 Place toasted pine nuts, basil, garlic and salt in food processor or blender. With processor running, add remaining ¼ cup oil in slow steady stream; process until evenly blended and pine nuts are finely chopped.

4 Transfer basil mixture to small bowl. Stir in Parmesan and Romano cheeses.*

5 Add pesto sauce to pasta; toss until well coated. Serve immediately.

*Pesto sauce can be stored at this point in airtight container; pour thin layer of olive oil over pesto and cover. Refrigerate up to 1 week. Bring to room temperature before using. Proceed as directed in step 5.

Makes 4 servings (about ¾ cup pesto sauce)

Sloppy Sloppy Joes

4 pounds ground beef

1 cup chopped onion

1 cup chopped green bell pepper

1 can (about 28 ounces) tomato sauce

2 cans (10¾ ounces each) condensed tomato soup, undiluted

1 cup packed brown sugar

¼ cup ketchup

3 tablespoons Worcestershire sauce

1 tablespoon ground mustard

1 tablespoon prepared mustard

1½ teaspoons chili powder

1 teaspoon garlic powder

Toasted sandwich rolls or hamburger buns

Slow Cooker Directions

1 Brown beef in large skillet over medium-high heat 6 to 8 minutes, stirring to break up meat. Drain fat. Add onion and bell pepper; cook 5 to 10 minutes, stirring frequently or until onion is translucent.

2 Transfer beef mixture to 4- to 5-quart slow cooker. Add tomato sauce, soup, brown sugar, ketchup, Worcesterhhire sauce, ground mustard, prepared mustard, chili powder and garlic powder; stir until well blended.

3 Cover; cook on LOW 4 to 6 hours. Serve on rolls.

Makes 20 to 25 servings

Easy Parmesan Chicken

8 ounces mushrooms, sliced

1 medium onion, cut into thin wedges

1 tablespoon olive oil

4 boneless skinless chicken breasts

1 jar (26 ounces) pasta sauce

½ teaspoon dried basil

¼ teaspoon dried oregano

1 bay leaf

½ cup (2 ounces) shredded part-skim mozzarella cheese

¼ cup grated Parmesan cheese

Hot cooked spaghetti

Slow Cooker Directions

1 Place mushrooms and onion in slow cooker.

2 Heat oil in large skillet over medium-high heat. Lightly brown chicken on both sides. Place chicken in slow cooker. Pour pasta sauce over chicken; add basil, oregano and bay leaf. Cover; cook on LOW 6 to 7 hours or on HIGH 3 to 4 hours or until chicken is tender. Remove and discard bay leaf.

3 Sprinkle chicken with cheeses. Cook, uncovered, on LOW 15 to 30 minutes or until cheeses are melted. Serve over spaghetti.

Makes 4 servings

Note: Other vegetables, such as sliced zucchini, cubed eggplant or broccoli florets, can be substituted for the mushroom slices.

Creamy Cheese and Macaroni

1½ cups uncooked elbow
    macaroni

1 cup chopped onion

1 cup chopped red or
    green bell pepper

¾ cup chopped celery

1 cup cottage cheese

1 cup (4 ounces) shredded
    Swiss cheese

½ cup shredded
    processed American
    cheese

½ cup milk

3 egg whites

3 tablespoons
    all-purpose flour

1 tablespoon margarine

¼ teaspoon black pepper

¼ teaspoon hot pepper
    sauce

1 Preheat oven to 350°F. Spray 2-quart casserole with nonstick cooking spray. Cook macaroni according to package directions, omitting salt. During last 5 minutes of cooking, add onion, bell pepper and celery. Drain macaroni and vegetables.

2 Combine cottage cheese, Swiss cheese, American cheese, milk, egg whites, flour, margarine, black pepper and hot pepper sauce in food processor or blender; process until smooth. Stir cheese mixture into macaroni and vegetables.

3 Pour mixture into prepared casserole. Bake 35 to 40 minutes or until golden brown. Let stand 10 minutes before serving.

Makes 4 servings

Beef & Noodles

1 tablespoon vegetable
   oil

2 pounds cubed beef
   stew meat

¼ pound mushrooms,
   sliced into halves

2 tablespoons chopped
   onion

2 cloves garlic, minced

1 teaspoon salt

1 teaspoon dried oregano

½ teaspoon black pepper

¼ teaspoon dried
   marjoram

1 bay leaf

1½ cups beef broth

⅓ cup dry sherry

1 cup (8 ounces) sour
   cream

½ cup all-purpose flour

¼ cup water

4 cups hot cooked
   noodles

Slow Cooker Directions

1 Heat oil in large skillet. Brown beef on all sides. (Work in batches, if necessary.) Drain and discard fat.

2 Combine beef, mushrooms, onion, garlic, salt, oregano, pepper, marjoram and bay leaf in slow cooker. Pour in broth and sherry. Cover; cook on LOW 8 to 10 hours or on HIGH 4 to 5 hours. Remove and discard bay leaf.

3 Combine sour cream, flour and water in small bowl. Stir about 1 cup liquid from slow cooker into sour cream mixture. Add mixture to slow cooker. Cook, uncovered, on HIGH 30 minutes or until thickened and bubbly. Serve over noodles. Garnish as desired.

Makes 8 servings

Chicken Caesar Salad

4 small boneless skinless chicken breasts

6 ounces uncooked gnocchi or other dried pasta

1 package (9 ounces) frozen artichoke hearts, thawed

1½ cups cherry tomatoes, quartered

¼ cup plus 2 tablespoons plain nonfat yogurt

2 tablespoons reduced-fat mayonnaise

2 tablespoons grated Romano cheese

1 tablespoon sherry or red wine vinegar

1 clove garlic, minced

½ teaspoon anchovy paste

½ teaspoon Dijon mustard

½ teaspoon white pepper

1 small head romaine lettuce, torn into bite-size pieces

1 cup toasted bread cubes or croutons

1 Grill or broil chicken breasts until no longer pink in center; set aside.

2 Cook pasta according to package directions, omitting salt. Drain and rinse well under cold running water until pasta is cool; drain well. Combine pasta, artichoke hearts and tomatoes in large bowl; set aside.

3 Combine yogurt, mayonnaise, Romano cheese, sherry, garlic, anchovy paste, mustard and pepper in small bowl; whisk until smooth. Add to pasta mixture; toss to coat evenly.

4 Arrange lettuce on platter or individual plates. Spoon pasta mixture over lettuce. Thinly slice chicken breasts and place on top of pasta. Sprinkle with bread cubes.

Makes 4 servings

Island Fish Tacos

Coleslaw

- 1 medium jicama (about 12 ounces), peeled and shredded
- 2 cups packaged coleslaw mix
- 3 tablespoons finely chopped fresh cilantro
- ¼ cup lime juice
- ¼ cup vegetable oil
- 3 tablespoons white vinegar
- 2 tablespoons mayonnaise
- 1 tablespoon honey
- 1 teaspoon salt

Salsa

- 2 medium tomatoes, diced (about 2 cups)
- ½ cup finely chopped red onion
- ¼ cup finely chopped fresh cilantro
- 2 tablespoons lime juice
- 2 tablespoons minced jalapeño pepper
- 1 teaspoon salt

Tacos

- 1 to 1¼ pounds white fish such as tilapia or mahi mahi, cut into 3×1½-inch pieces
- Salt and black pepper
- 2 tablespoons vegetable oil
- 12 taco-size tortillas (6 inches), heated
- Guacamole (optional)

1 For coleslaw, combine jicama, coleslaw mix and 3 tablespoons cilantro in medium bowl. Whisk ¼ cup lime juice, ¼ cup oil, vinegar, mayonnaise, honey and 1 teaspoon salt in small bowl until well blended. Pour over vegetable mixture; stir to coat. Let stand at least 15 minutes for flavors to blend.

2 For salsa, place tomatoes in fine-mesh strainer; set in bowl or sink to drain 15 minutes. Transfer to another medium bowl. Stir in onion, ¼ cup cilantro, 2 tablespoons lime juice, jalapeño pepper and 1 teaspoon salt; mix well.

3 For tacos, season both sides of fish with salt and black pepper. Heat 1 tablespoon oil in large nonstick skillet over medium-high heat. Add half of fish; cook about 2 minutes per side or until fish is opaque and begins to flake when tested with fork. Repeat with remaining oil and fish.

4 Serve fish in tortillas with coleslaw and salsa. Serve with guacamole, if desired.

Makes 4 servings

BLT Supreme

12 to 16 slices thick-cut bacon

⅓ cup mayonnaise

1½ teaspoons minced chipotle peppers in adobo sauce

1 teaspoon lime juice

1 ripe avocado

⅛ teaspoon salt

⅛ teaspoon black pepper

4 leaves romaine lettuce

½ baguette, cut into 2 (8-inch) lengths or 2 hoagie rolls, split and toasted

6 to 8 slices tomato

1 Cook bacon in skillet or oven until crisp-chewy. Drain on paper towel-lined plate.

2 Meanwhile, combine mayonnaise, chipotle peppers and lime juice in small bowl; mix well. Coarsely mash avocado in another small bowl; stir in salt and pepper. Cut romaine leaves crosswise into ¼-inch strips.

3 For each sandwich, spread heaping tablespoon mayonnaise mixture on bottom half of baguette; top with one fourth of lettuce. Arrange 3 to 4 slices bacon over lettuce; spread 2 tablespoons mashed avocado over bacon. Drizzle with heaping tablespoon mayonnaise mixture. Top with 3 to 4 tomato slices, one fourth of lettuce and 3 to 4 slices bacon. Close sandwich with top half of baguette.

Makes 2 servings

Parmesan-Crusted Tilapia

⅔ cup plus 3 tablespoons grated Parmesan cheese, divided

⅔ cup panko bread crumbs

⅓ cup prepared Alfredo sauce (refrigerated or jarred)

1½ teaspoons dried parsley flakes

4 tilapia fillets (6 ounces each)

Shaved Parmesan cheese (optional)

Minced fresh parsley (optional)

1 Preheat oven to 425°F. Line baking sheet with foil; spray foil with nonstick cooking spray.

2 Combine ⅔ cup grated cheese and panko in medium bowl; mix well. Combine Alfredo sauce, remaining 3 tablespoons grated cheese and parsley flakes in small bowl; mix well. Spread sauce mixture over top of fish fillets, coating in thick, even layer. Top with panko mixture, pressing in gently to adhere. Place fish on prepared baking sheet.

3 Bake on top rack of oven about 15 minutes or until crust is golden brown and fish begins to flake when tested with fork. Garnish with shaved Parmesan and fresh parsley.

Makes 4 servings

Eggplant Parmesan

2 tablespoons olive oil

2 cloves garlic, minced

1 can (28 ounces) Italian whole tomatoes, undrained

½ cup water

1¼ teaspoons salt, divided

¼ teaspoon dried oregano

Pinch red pepper flakes

1 medium eggplant (about 1 pound)

⅓ cup all-purpose flour

¼ teaspoon black pepper

⅔ cup milk

1 egg

1 cup Italian-seasoned dry bread crumbs

4 to 5 tablespoons vegetable oil, divided

1 cup (4 ounces) shredded mozzarella cheese

Chopped fresh parsley

1 Heat olive oil in medium saucepan over medium heat. Add garlic; cook and stir 2 minutes or until softened (do not brown). Crush tomatoes with hands (in bowl or in can); add to saucepan with juices from can. Stir in water, 1 teaspoon salt, oregano and red pepper flakes; bring to a simmer. Reduce heat to medium-low; cook 45 minutes, stirring occasionally.

2 Meanwhile, prepare eggplant. Cut eggplant crosswise into ¼-inch slices. Combine flour, remaining ¼ teaspoon salt and black pepper in shallow dish. Beat milk and egg in another shallow dish. Place bread crumbs in third shallow dish.

3 Coat both sides eggplant slices with flour mixture, shaking off excess. Dip in egg mixture, letting excess drip back into dish. Roll in bread crumbs to coat.

4 Heat 3 tablespoons vegetable oil in large skillet over medium-high heat. Working in batches, add eggplant slices to skillet in single layer; cook 3 to 4 minutes per side or until golden brown, adding additional vegetable oil as needed. Remove to paper towel-lined plate; cover loosely with foil to keep warm.

5 Preheat broiler. Spray 13×9-inch baking dish with nonstick cooking spray. Arrange eggplant slices overlapping in baking dish; top with half of warm marinara sauce. (Reserve remaining marinara sauce for pasta or another use.) Sprinkle with cheese.

6 Broil 2 to 3 minutes or just until cheese is melted and beginning to brown. Garnish with parsley.

Makes 4 servings

Chicken Waldorf Salad

Dressing

- ⅓ cup balsamic vinegar
- 2 tablespoons Dijon mustard
- 2 teaspoons minced garlic
- ½ teaspoon salt
- ¼ teaspoon black pepper
- ⅔ cup extra virgin olive oil

Salad

- 8 cups mixed greens
- 1 large Granny Smith apple, cut into ½-inch pieces
- ⅔ cup diced celery
- ⅔ cup halved red seedless grapes
- 12 to 16 ounces sliced grilled chicken breasts
- ½ cup candied walnuts
- ½ cup crumbled blue cheese

1 For dressing, combine vinegar, mustard, garlic, salt and pepper in medium bowl; mix well. Slowly add oil, whisking until well blended.

2 For salad, combine mixed greens, apple, celery and grapes in large bowl. Add half of dressing; toss to coat. Top with chicken, walnuts and cheese; drizzle with additional dressing.

Makes 4 servings

Tuna Melts

1 can (12 ounces) chunk white tuna packed in water, drained and flaked

1½ cups packaged coleslaw mix

3 tablespoons sliced green onions

3 tablespoons mayonnaise

1 tablespoon Dijon mustard

1 teaspoon dried dill weed (optional)

4 English muffins, split and lightly toasted

⅓ cup shredded Cheddar cheese

1 Preheat broiler. Combine tuna, coleslaw mix and green onions in medium bowl. Combine mayonnaise, mustard and dill weed, if desired, in small bowl. Stir mayonnaise mixture into tuna mixture. Spread tuna mixture onto muffin halves. Place on broiler pan.

2 Broil 4 inches from heat 3 to 4 minutes or until heated through. Sprinkle with cheese. Broil 1 to 2 minutes more or until cheese is melted.

Makes 4 servings

Cabbage Rolls

6 cups water

12 large cabbage leaves

1 pound lean ground lamb

½ cup cooked rice

1 teaspoon salt

¼ teaspoon dried oregano

¼ teaspoon ground nutmeg

¼ teaspoon black pepper

1½ cups tomato sauce

Slow Cooker Directions

1 Bring water to a boil in large saucepan. Turn off heat. Soak cabbage leaves in water 5 minutes; remove, drain and cool leaves.

2 Combine lamb, rice, salt, oregano, nutmeg and pepper in large bowl; mix well. Place 2 tablespoonfuls mixture in center of each cabbage leaf; roll up firmly. Place cabbage rolls in slow cooker, seam side down. Pour tomato sauce over cabbage rolls.

3 Cover; cook on LOW 8 to 10 hours.

Makes 6 servings

Authentic Meat Loaf

¾ cup tomato sauce, divided

2 egg whites

4 tablespoons chunky salsa, divided

½ teaspoon black pepper

½ cup old-fashioned oats

½ cup finely minced onion

⅓ cup canned mushroom stems and pieces, drained and chopped

1 clove garlic, finely minced

8 ounces lean ground turkey

8 ounces lean ground beef

1 Preheat oven to 350°F. Spray piece of foil with nonstick cooking spray. Place foil on broiler pan; set aside.

2 Mix ½ cup tomato sauce, egg whites, 3 tablespoons salsa and pepper in medium bowl. Stir in oats, onion, mushrooms and garlic.

3 Place ground turkey and ground beef in large bowl; mix lightly to combine. Stir in tomato mixture; mix well.

4 Transfer meat mixture to prepared pan; shape into 8×4-inch rectangular loaf. Mix remaining ¼ cup tomato sauce and 1 tablespoon salsa in small bowl; drizzle on top of meat loaf.

5 Bake 55 minutes or until cooked through (165°F). Let stand 5 minutes before slicing.

Makes 4 servings

Side Dishes

Smashed Potatoes

4 medium russet potatoes (about 1½ pounds), peeled and cut into ¼-inch cubes

⅓ cup milk

2 tablespoons sour cream

1 tablespoon minced onion

½ teaspoon salt

¼ teaspoon black pepper

⅛ teaspoon garlic powder (optional)

Chopped fresh chives or French fried onions (optional)

1 Bring large saucepan of lightly salted water to a boil. Add potatoes; cook 15 to 20 minutes or until fork-tender. Drain and return to saucepan.

2 Slightly mash potatoes. Stir in milk, sour cream, minced onion, salt, pepper and garlic powder, if desired. Mash until desired texture is reached, leaving potatoes chunky. Cook 5 minutes over low heat or until heated through, stirring occasionally. Top with chives, if desired.

Makes 4 servings

Chicken Fried Rice

2 tablespoons vegetable oil, divided

12 ounces boneless skinless chicken breasts, cut into ½-inch cubes

Salt and black pepper

2 tablespoons butter

2 cloves garlic, minced

½ sweet onion, diced

1 medium carrot, diced

2 green onions, thinly sliced

3 eggs

4 cups cooked rice*

3 tablespoons soy sauce

2 tablespoons sesame seeds

*For rice, cook 1½ cups rice according to package directions without oil or butter. Spread hot rice on large rimmed baking sheet; cool to room temperature. Refrigerate several hours or overnight.

1 Heat 1 tablespoon oil in large skillet over medium-high heat. Add chicken; season with salt and pepper. Cook and stir 5 to 6 minutes or until cooked through. Add butter and garlic; cook and stir 1 minute or until butter is melted. Remove to small bowl.

2 Add sweet onion, carrot and green onions to skillet; cook and stir over high heat 3 minutes or until vegetables are softened. Add to bowl with chicken.

3 Heat remaining 1 tablespoon oil in same skillet. Crack eggs into skillet; cook and stir 45 seconds or until eggs are scrambled but still moist. Add chicken and vegetable mixture, rice, soy sauce and sesame seeds; cook and stir 2 minutes or until well blended and heated through. Season with additional salt and pepper.

Makes 4 servings

Coleslaw

1 medium head green
  cabbage, shredded

1 medium carrot,
  shredded

½ cup mayonnaise

½ cup milk

⅓ cup sugar

3 tablespoons lemon juice

1½ tablespoons white
  vinegar

½ teaspoon salt

⅛ teaspoon black pepper

1 Combine cabbage and carrot in large bowl; mix well.

2 Combine mayonnaise, milk, sugar, lemon juice, vinegar, salt and pepper in medium bowl; whisk until well blended. Add to cabbage mixture; stir until blended.

Makes 10 servings

Garlic Knots

¾ cup warm water (105° to 115°F)

1 package (¼ ounce) active dry yeast

1 teaspoon sugar

2¼ cups all-purpose flour

2 tablespoons olive oil, divided

1½ teaspoons salt, divided

4 tablespoons (½ stick) butter, divided

1 tablespoon minced garlic

¼ teaspoon garlic powder

½ cup grated Parmesan cheese

2 tablespoons chopped fresh parsley

½ teaspoon dried oregano

1 Combine water, yeast and sugar in large bowl of electric stand mixer; stir to dissolve yeast. Let stand 5 minutes or until bubbly. Stir in flour, 1 tablespoon oil and 1 teaspoon salt; knead with dough hook at low speed 5 minutes or until dough is smooth and elastic. Shape dough into a ball. Place in large lightly greased bowl; turn to grease top. Cover and let rise 1 hour or until doubled in size.

2 Melt 2 tablespoons butter in small saucepan over low heat. Add remaining 1 tablespoon oil, ½ teaspoon salt, minced garlic and garlic powder; cook over very low heat 5 minutes. Pour into small bowl; set aside.

3 Preheat oven to 400°F. Line baking sheet with parchment paper.

4 Turn out dough onto lightly floured surface. Punch down dough; let stand 10 minutes. Roll out dough into 10×8-inch rectangle. Cut into 20 (2-inch) squares. Roll each piece into 8-inch rope; tie in a knot. Place knots on prepared baking sheet; brush with garlic mixture.

5 Bake 10 minutes or until knots are lightly browned. Meanwhile, melt remaining 2 tablespoons butter. Combine cheese, parsley and oregano in small bowl; mix well. Brush melted butter over baked knots; immediately sprinkle with cheese mixture. Cool slightly; serve warm.

Makes 20 knots

Twice "Baked" Potatoes

4 baking potatoes (about 10 ounces *each*)

3 tablespoons olive oil, divided

1 head garlic

1 to 2 tablespoons milk

4 tablespoons sour cream

½ teaspoon salt

¼ teaspoon black pepper

2 slices bacon, cooked and chopped

½ cup (2 ounces) shredded Cheddar cheese, divided

¼ teaspoon smoked paprika

Chopped green onions (optional)

Slow Cooker Directions

1 Rub potatoes with 2 tablespoons oil; wrap each potato in foil. Place potatoes in slow cooker. Cut across top of garlic head. Place garlic in foil; top with remaining 1 tablespoon oil. Twist foil closed around garlic; place on top of potatoes. Cover; cook on HIGH 4 hours or until potatoes are soft when pierced with knife.

2 Pull foil away from each potato; crimp it around bottom of potatoes. Cut thin slice from top of each potato. Scoop inside of potatoes into large bowl, leaving about ¼-inch shell. Squeeze garlic head to remove softened cloves; mash with fork. Measure 1 tablespoon mashed garlic; add to large bowl with potatoes. Refrigerate remaining garlic in airtight jar for another use.

3 Add milk, sour cream, salt and pepper to large bowl with potatoes; beat with electric mixer at medium speed 3 to 4 minutes or until smooth. Stir in bacon and half of cheese. Spoon mashed potatoes into shells, mounding at top. Top with remaining cheese and paprika. Return potatoes to slow cooker. Cover; cook on HIGH 15 minutes or until cheese is melted. Garnish with green onions.

Makes 4 servings

Simple Golden Cornbread

1¼ cups all-purpose flour

¾ cup yellow cornmeal

⅓ cup sugar

2 teaspoons baking powder

1 teaspoon salt

1¼ cups whole milk

¼ cup (½ stick) butter, melted

1 egg

Honey Butter (recipe follows, optional)

1 Preheat oven to 400°F. Spray 8-inch square baking dish or pan with nonstick cooking spray.

2 Combine flour, cornmeal, sugar, baking powder and salt in large bowl; mix well. Beat milk, butter and egg in medium bowl until well blended. Add to flour mixture; stir just until dry ingredients are moistened. Pour batter into prepared baking dish.

3 Bake about 25 minutes or until golden brown and toothpick inserted into center comes out clean. Prepare Honey Butter, if desired. Serve with cornbread.

Makes 9 to 12 servings

Honey Butter: Beat 6 tablespoons (¾ stick) softened butter and ¼ cup honey in medium bowl with electric mixer at medium-high speed until light and creamy.

Steakhouse Creamed Spinach

1 pound baby spinach

½ cup (1 stick) butter

2 tablespoons finely chopped onion

¼ cup all-purpose flour

2 cups whole milk

1 bay leaf

½ teaspoon salt

Pinch ground nutmeg

Pinch ground red pepper

Black pepper

1 Heat medium saucepan of water to a boil over high heat. Add spinach; cook 1 minute. Drain and transfer to bowl of ice water to stop cooking. Squeeze spinach dry; coarsely chop. Wipe out saucepan with paper towel.

2 Melt butter in same saucepan over medium heat. Add onion; cook and stir 2 minutes or until softened. Add flour; cook and stir 2 to 3 minutes or until slightly golden. Slowly add milk in thin, steady stream, whisking constantly until mixture boils and begins to thicken. Stir in bay leaf, ½ teaspoon salt, nutmeg and red pepper. Reduce heat to low; cook 5 minutes, stirring frequently. Remove and discard bay leaf.

3 Stir in spinach; cook 5 minutes, stirring frequently. Season with additional salt and black pepper.

Makes 4 servings

Soft Garlic Breadsticks

1½ cups water

6 tablespoons (¾ stick) butter, divided

4 cups all-purpose flour

2 tablespoons sugar

1 package (¼ ounce) active dry yeast

1½ teaspoons salt

¾ teaspoon coarse salt

¼ teaspoon garlic powder

1 Heat water and 2 tablespoons butter in small saucepan or microwavable bowl to 110° to 115°F. (Butter does not need to melt completely.)

2 Combine flour, sugar, yeast and 1½ teaspoons salt in large bowl of stand mixer; beat at low speed to combine. Add water mixture; beat until dough begins to come together. Knead at low speed with dough hook about 5 minutes or until dough is smooth and elastic. Shape dough into a ball. Place in large greased bowl; turn to grease top. Cover and let rise in warm place about 1 hour or until doubled in size.

3 Line two baking sheets with parchment paper or spray with nonstick cooking spray. Punch down dough. For each breadstick, pull off piece of dough slightly larger than a golf ball (about 2 ounces) and roll between hands or on work surface into 7-inch-long stick. Place on prepared baking sheets; cover loosely and let rise in warm place about 45 minutes or until doubled in size.

4 Preheat oven to 400°F. Melt remaining 4 tablespoons butter in small bowl. Brush breadsticks with 2 tablespoons butter; sprinkle with coarse salt.

5 Bake breadsticks 13 to 15 minutes or until golden brown. Stir garlic powder into remaining 2 tablespoons melted butter; brush over breadsticks immediately after removing from oven. Serve warm.

Makes about 16 breadsticks

Super Simple Cheesy Bubble Loaf

2 packages (7½ ounces each) refrigerated buttermilk biscuits (10 biscuits per package)

2 tablespoons butter, melted

1½ cups (6 ounces) shredded Italian cheese blend

1 Preheat oven to 350°F. Spray 9×5-inch loaf pan with nonstick cooking spray.

2 Separate biscuits; cut each biscuit into four pieces with scissors. Layer half of biscuit pieces in prepared pan. Drizzle with 1 tablespoon butter; sprinkle with 1 cup cheese. Top with remaining biscuit pieces, 1 tablespoon butter and ½ cup cheese.

3 Bake about 25 minutes or until golden brown. Serve warm.

Makes 12 servings

Tip: It's easy to change up the flavors in this simple bread. Try Mexican cheese blend instead of Italian, and add taco seasoning and/or hot pepper sauce to the melted butter before drizzling it over the dough. Or, sprinkle ¼ cup chopped ham, salami or crumbled crisp-cooked bacon between the layers of dough.

Spinach Salad

Dressing

- ¼ cup balsamic vinegar
- 1 clove garlic, minced
- ½ teaspoon sugar
- ¼ teaspoon salt
- ⅛ teaspoon black pepper
- ¼ cup olive oil
- ¼ cup vegetable oil

Salad

- 8 cups packed baby spinach
- 1 cup diced tomatoes (about 2 medium)
- 1 cup drained mandarin oranges
- 1 cup glazed pecans*
- ½ cup crumbled feta cheese
- ½ cup diced red onion
- ½ cup dried cranberries
- 1 can (3 ounces) crispy rice noodles**
- 4 teaspoons toasted sesame seeds

*Glazed pecans can be found in the produce section of many supermarkets (with other salad toppings). If unavailable, they can be prepared easily at home. (See Tip.)

**Crispy rice noodles can be found with canned chow mein noodles in the Asian section of the supermarket.

1 For dressing, whisk vinegar, garlic, sugar, salt and pepper in medium bowl until blended. Whisk in olive oil and vegetable oil in thin, steady stream until well blended.

2 Divide spinach among four serving bowls. Top evenly with tomatoes, oranges, pecans, cheese, onion and cranberries. Sprinkle with rice noodles and sesame seeds. Drizzle each salad with 3 tablespoons dressing.

Makes 4 servings

Tip: To make glazed pecans, combine 1 cup pecan halves, ¼ cup sugar, 1 tablespoon butter and ½ teaspoon salt in medium skillet; cook and stir over medium heat 5 minutes or until sugar mixture is dark brown and nuts are well coated. Spread on large plate; cool completely. Break into pieces or coarsely chop.

Cheesy Garlic Bread

1 loaf (about 16 ounces) Italian bread

½ cup (1 stick) butter, softened

8 cloves garlic, very thinly sliced

¼ cup grated Parmesan cheese

2 cups (8 ounces) shredded mozzarella cheese

1 Preheat oven to 425°F. Line large baking sheet with foil.

2 Cut bread in half horizontally. Spread cut sides of bread evenly with butter; top with sliced garlic. Sprinkle with Parmesan, then mozzarella cheeses. Place on prepared baking sheet.

3 Bake 12 minutes or until cheeses are melted and golden brown in spots. Cut crosswise into slices. Serve warm.

Makes 8 to 10 servings

Potato Skins

8 medium baking
   potatoes (6 to
   8 ounces each)

1 tablespoon vegetable
   oil

1 teaspoon salt

⅛ teaspoon black pepper

1 tablespoon butter,
   melted

1 cup (4 ounces) shredded
   Cheddar cheese

8 slices bacon, crisp-
   cooked and coarsely
   chopped

1 cup sour cream

3 tablespoons snipped
   fresh chives

1 Preheat oven to 400°F.

2 Prick potatoes all over with fork. Rub oil over potatoes;
  sprinkle with salt and pepper. Place in 13×9-inch baking
  pan. Bake 1 hour or until fork-tender. Let stand until cool
  enough to handle. *Reduce oven temperature to 350°F.*

3 Cut potatoes in half lengthwise; cut small slice off bottom
  of each half so potato halves lay flat. Scoop out soft
  middles of potato skins; reserve for another use. Place
  potato halves skin sides up in baking pan; brush potato
  skins with butter.

4 Bake 20 to 25 minutes or until crisp. Turn potatoes over;
  top with cheese and bacon. Bake 5 minutes or until
  cheese is melted. Cool slightly. Top with sour cream and
  chives just before serving.

Makes 6 to 8 servings

Desserts

Chocolate Chip Cookies

1¼ cups all-purpose flour

½ teaspoon salt

½ teaspoon baking soda

½ cup (1 stick) butter, softened

½ cup granulated sugar

¼ cup packed brown sugar

1 egg

1 teaspoon vanilla

1 cup semisweet or bittersweet chocolate chips

Coarse salt or flaky sea salt

1 Preheat oven to 350°F. Line cookie sheets with parchment paper.

2 Combine flour, ½ teaspoon salt and baking soda in medium bowl.

3 Beat butter, granulated sugar and brown sugar in large bowl with electric mixer at medium speed until light and fluffy. Add egg and vanilla; beat until well blended. Add flour mixture; beat just until blended. Stir in chocolate chips. Drop tablespoonfuls of dough 2 inches apart onto prepared cookie sheets. Sprinkle tops with coarse salt.

4 Bake 10 to 12 minutes or until edges are lightly browned. Cool on cookie sheets 1 minute. Remove to wire racks; cool completely.

Makes about 2 dozen cookies

Note: For best flavor, wrap dough in plastic wrap and refrigerate overnight or up to 2 days.

Warm Apple Crostata

1¾ cups all-purpose flour

⅓ cup granulated sugar

½ teaspoon plus ⅛ teaspoon salt, divided

¾ cup (1½ sticks) cold butter, cut into small pieces

3 tablespoons ice water

2 teaspoons vanilla

8 Pink Lady or Honeycrisp apples (about 1½ pounds), peeled and cut into ¼-inch slices

¼ cup packed brown sugar

1 tablespoon lemon juice

1 teaspoon ground cinnamon

⅛ teaspoon ground nutmeg

4 teaspoons butter, cut into very small pieces

1 egg, beaten

1 to 2 teaspoons coarse sugar

Vanilla ice cream

Caramel sauce or ice cream topping

1 Combine flour, granulated sugar and ½ teaspoon salt in food processor; process 5 seconds. Add ¾ cup butter; process about 10 seconds or until mixture resembles coarse crumbs.

2 Combine ice water and vanilla in small bowl. With motor running, pour mixture through feed tube; process 12 seconds or until dough begins to come together. Shape dough into a disc; wrap in plastic wrap and refrigerate 30 minutes.

3 Meanwhile, combine apples, brown sugar, lemon juice, cinnamon, nutmeg and remaining ⅛ teaspoon salt in large bowl; toss to coat. Preheat oven to 400°F.

4 Line two baking sheets with parchment paper. Cut dough into four pieces; roll out each piece into 7-inch circle on floured surface. Place on prepared baking sheets; mound apples in center of dough circles (about 1 cup apples for each crostata). Fold or roll up edges of dough towards center to create rim of crostata. Dot apples with 4 teaspoons butter. Brush dough with egg; sprinkle dough and apples with coarse sugar.

5 Bake about 20 minutes or until apples are tender and crust is golden brown. Serve warm topped with ice cream and caramel sauce.

Makes 4 tarts

Key Lime Pie

12 whole graham crackers*

⅓ cup butter, melted

3 tablespoons sugar

2 cans (14 ounces each) sweetened condensed milk

¾ cup key lime juice

6 egg yolks

Pinch salt

Whipped cream (optional)

Lime slices (optional)

*Or substitute 1½ cups graham cracker crumbs.

1 Preheat oven to 350°F. Spray 9-inch pie plate or springform pan with nonstick cooking spray.

2 Place graham crackers in food processor; pulse until coarse crumbs form. Add butter and sugar; pulse until well blended. Press mixture onto bottom and 1 inch up side of prepared pie plate. Bake 8 minutes or until lightly browned. Remove to wire rack to cool 10 minutes. *Reduce oven temperature to 325°F.*

3 Meanwhile, beat sweetened condensed milk, lime juice, egg yolks and salt in large bowl with electric mixer at medium-low speed 1 minute or until well blended and smooth. Pour into crust.

4 Bake 20 minutes or until top is set. Cool completely in pan on wire rack. Cover and refrigerate 2 hours or overnight. Garnish with whipped cream and lime slices.

Makes 8 servings

Cinnamon Apples

¼ cup (½ stick) butter

3 tart red apples such as Gala, Fuji or Honeycrisp (about 1½ pounds total), peeled and cut into ½-inch wedges

¼ cup packed brown sugar

1 teaspoon ground cinnamon

⅛ teaspoon ground nutmeg

⅛ teaspoon salt

1 tablespoon cornstarch

1 Melt butter in large skillet over medium-high heat. Add apples; cook about 8 minutes or until apples are tender, stirring occasionally.

2 Add brown sugar, cinnamon, nutmeg and salt; cook and stir 1 minute or until glazed. Reduce heat to medium-low; stir in cornstarch until well blended.

3 Remove from heat; let stand 5 minutes for glaze to thicken. Stir again; serve immediately.

Makes 4 servings

Chocolate Peanut Butter Pie

10 whole chocolate graham crackers, broken into pieces

2 tablespoons granulated sugar

¼ cup (½ stick) butter, melted

1 package (8 ounces) cream cheese, softened

1 cup creamy peanut butter

1¾ cups powdered sugar, divided

3 tablespoons butter, softened

1¾ teaspoons vanilla, divided

¼ teaspoon salt

2 cups cold whipping cream

½ cup unsweetened cocoa powder

2 packages (1½ ounces each) chocolate peanut butter cups, chopped

Hot fudge sauce, heated (optional)

1 Preheat oven to 350°F. Combine graham crackers and granulated sugar in food processor; process until finely ground. Add ¼ cup melted butter; process until well blended. Press into bottom and up side of 9-inch pie plate.

2 Bake 8 minutes. Cool completely on wire rack.

3 Meanwhile, beat cream cheese, peanut butter, ¾ cup powdered sugar, 3 tablespoons softened butter, 1 teaspoon vanilla and salt in large bowl with electric mixer at medium speed about 3 minutes or until light and fluffy. Spread filling in cooled crust; smooth top. Refrigerate pie while preparing topping.

4 Beat cream, remaining 1 cup powdered sugar, ¾ teaspoon vanilla and cocoa in medium bowl with electric mixer at high speed 1 to 2 minutes or until soft peaks form. Spread chocolate whipped cream over peanut butter layer; sprinkle with peanut butter cups. Refrigerate several hours or overnight.

5 Drizzle serving plates with hot fudge sauce, if desired. Serve pie over sauce.

Makes 8 servings

Carrot Cake

Cake

- 2 cups all-purpose flour
- 2 teaspoons baking soda
- 2 teaspoons ground cinnamon
- 1 teaspoon salt
- 4 eggs
- 2¼ cups granulated sugar
- 1 cup vegetable oil
- 1 cup buttermilk
- 1 tablespoon vanilla
- 3 medium carrots, shredded (3 cups)
- 3 cups walnuts, chopped and toasted, divided
- 1 cup shredded coconut
- 1 can (8 ounces) crushed pineapple

Frosting

- 2 packages (8 ounces each) cream cheese, softened
- 1 cup (2 sticks) butter, softened
- Pinch salt
- 3 cups powdered sugar
- 1 tablespoon orange juice
- 2 teaspoons grated orange peel
- 1 teaspoon vanilla

1 Preheat oven to 350°F. Spray two 9-inch round cake pans with nonstick cooking spray. Line bottoms of pans with parchment paper; spray with cooking spray.

2 For cake, combine flour, baking soda, cinnamon and 1 teaspoon salt in medium bowl; mix well. Whisk eggs in large bowl until blended. Add granulated sugar, oil, buttermilk and 1 tablespoon vanilla; whisk until well blended. Add flour mixture; stir until well blended. Add carrots, 1 cup walnuts, coconut and pineapple; stir just until blended. Pour batter into prepared pans.

3 Bake 25 to 30 minutes or until toothpick inserted into centers comes out clean. Cool in pans 10 minutes; remove to wire racks to cool completely.

4 For frosting, beat cream cheese, butter and pinch of salt in large bowl with electric mixer at medium speed 3 minutes or until creamy. Add powdered sugar, orange juice, orange peel and 1 teaspoon vanilla; beat at low speed until blended. Beat at medium speed 2 minutes or until frosting is smooth.

5 Place one cake layer on serving plate. Top with 2 cups frosting; spread evenly. Top with second cake layer; frost top and side of cake with remaining frosting. Press 1¾ cups walnuts onto side of cake. Sprinkle remaining ¼ cup walnuts over top of cake.

Makes 8 to 10 servings

Warm Chocolate Soufflé Cakes

6 tablespoons (¾ stick) butter

4 ounces semisweet chocolate

½ cup granulated sugar

1½ tablespoons cornstarch

⅛ teaspoon salt

2 eggs

2 egg yolks

Raspberry Sauce (optional, recipe follows)

Powdered sugar

1 Spray four 6-ounce ramekins with nonstick cooking spray. Place on small baking sheet.

2 Combine butter and chocolate in small saucepan; heat over low heat until mixture is melted and smooth, stirring frequently. Combine granulated sugar, cornstarch and salt in medium bowl; mix well. Add chocolate mixture to sugar mixture; whisk until well blended.

3 Whisk eggs and egg yolks in small bowl. Add to sugar mixture; whisk just until blended. Divide evenly among prepared ramekins; cover and refrigerate overnight. Prepare Raspberry Sauce, if desired.

4 Preheat oven to 375°F. Bake 18 to 20 minutes or just until cakes are barely set (batter does not jiggle or look shiny). Sprinkle with powdered sugar; serve with Raspberry Sauce.

Makes 4 servings

Raspberry Sauce: Combine 1 (12-ounce) package thawed frozen raspberries and ¼ cup granulated sugar in food processor or blender; process until smooth. Press through fine-mesh sieve to remove seeds.

Sweet Potato Pecan Pie

1 sweet potato (about
  1 pound)

3 eggs, divided

8 tablespoons granulated
  sugar, divided

8 tablespoons packed
  brown sugar, divided

2 tablespoons butter,
  melted, divided

½ teaspoon ground
  cinnamon

½ teaspoon salt, divided

1 frozen 9-inch deep-dish
  pie crust

½ cup dark corn syrup

1½ teaspoons vanilla

1½ teaspoons lemon juice

1 cup pecan halves

  Vanilla ice cream
  (optional)

1 Preheat oven to 350°F. Prick sweet potato with fork. Bake 1 hour or until fork-tender; let stand until cool enough to handle. Peel sweet potato; place in bowl of electric stand mixer. *Reduce oven temperature to 300°F.*

2 Add 1 egg, 2 tablespoons granulated sugar, 2 tablespoons brown sugar, 1 tablespoon butter, cinnamon and ¼ teaspoon salt to bowl with sweet potato; beat at medium speed 5 minutes or until smooth and fluffy. Spread mixture in frozen crust; place in refrigerator.

3 Combine corn syrup, remaining 6 tablespoons granulated sugar, 6 tablespoons brown sugar, 1 tablespoon butter, vanilla, lemon juice and remaining ¼ teaspoon salt in clean mixer bowl; beat at medium speed 5 minutes. Add remaining 2 eggs; beat 5 minutes. Place crust on baking sheet. Spread pecans over sweet potato filling; pour corn syrup mixture evenly over pecans.

4 Bake 1 hour or until center is set and top is deep golden brown. Cool completely. Serve with ice cream, if desired.

Makes 8 servings

Chocolate Chunk Pizza Cookie

2 cups all-purpose flour

1 teaspoon baking soda

1 teaspoon salt

¾ cup (1½ sticks) butter, softened

1 cup packed brown sugar

¼ cup granulated sugar

2 eggs

1 teaspoon vanilla

1 package (about 11 ounces) chocolate chunks

Vanilla ice cream

1 Preheat oven to 400°F. Spray three 6-inch cast iron skillets, cake pans or deep-dish pizza pans with nonstick cooking spray.*

2 Combine flour, baking soda and salt in medium bowl; mix well. Beat butter, brown sugar and granulated sugar in large bowl with electric mixer at medium speed until creamy. Beat in eggs and vanilla until well blended. Gradually beat in flour mixture at low speed just until blended. Stir in chocolate chunks. Spread dough evenly in prepared pans.

3 Bake about 15 minutes or until top and edges are deep golden brown but center is still slightly soft. Top with ice cream. Serve warm.

If you don't have three skillets or pans, you can bake one cookie at a time. Refrigerate the dough between batches and make sure the skillet is completely cool before adding more dough. (Clean and spray the skillet again before adding each new batch.)

Makes 3 pizza cookies

Apple & Cherry Pie

2 cups all-purpose flour

½ cup plus 2½ tablespoons sugar, divided

½ teaspoon salt

3 tablespoons margarine or butter

3 tablespoons shortening

1 tablespoon cider vinegar

5 to 6 tablespoons ice water

½ cup dried cherries

¼ cup apple juice

1 tablespoon cornstarch

2¼ teaspoons ground cinnamon, divided

6 cups sliced peeled apples, preferably Jonagold or Golden Delicious

1 teaspoon vanilla

1 egg white, well beaten

1 Combine flour, 2 tablespoons sugar and salt in medium bowl. Cut in margarine and shortening with pastry blender or two knives until mixture resembles coarse crumbs. Add vinegar and 4 tablespoons water, stirring with fork. Add additional water, 1 tablespoon at a time, until mixture forms dough. Divide dough into thirds. Shape one piece into a disc; wrap in plastic wrap. Combine remaining two pieces to form a larger disc; wrap in plastic wrap. Refrigerate 30 minutes.

2 Preheat oven to 375°F. Combine cherries and apple juice in small microwavable bowl; microwave on HIGH 1½ minutes. Let stand 15 minutes. Combine ½ cup sugar, cornstarch and 2 teaspoons cinnamon in large bowl. Add apples and vanilla; toss to combine.

3 Coat 9-inch pie plate with nonstick cooking spray. Roll larger disc of dough into 12-inch circle on floured surface. Line prepared pie plate. Spoon apple mixture into crust. Roll smaller disc of dough into 10-inch circle. Cut into ½-inch strips. Arrange in lattice design over fruit. Seal and flute edge; brush with egg white. Combine remaining ½ tablespoon sugar and ¼ teaspoon cinnamon in small bowl; sprinkle over pie.

4 Bake 45 minutes or until apples are tender and crust is golden brown. Cool on wire rack 30 minutes. Serve warm or at room temperature.

Makes 8 servings

Tip: If the pie crust is browning too quickly, cover the edges with strips of foil. An alternative is to cut the bottom out of another foil pie pan and invert it over the pie.

Mexican Wedding Cookies

1 cup pecan pieces or halves

1 cup (2 sticks) butter, softened

2 cups powdered sugar, divided

2 cups all-purpose flour

2 teaspoons vanilla

⅛ teaspoon salt

1 Place pecans in food processor; process using on/off pulses until pecans are ground but not pasty.

2 Beat butter and ½ cup powdered sugar in large bowl with electric mixer at medium speed until light and fluffy. Gradually add 1 cup flour, vanilla and salt; beat at low speed until well blended. Stir in remaining 1 cup flour and ground nuts. Shape dough into a ball; wrap in plastic wrap. Refrigerate 1 hour or until firm.

3 Preheat oven to 350°F. Shape dough into 1-inch balls. Place 1 inch apart on ungreased cookie sheets.

4 Bake 12 to 15 minutes or until golden brown. Cool on cookie sheets 2 minutes.

5 Meanwhile, place 1 cup powdered sugar in 13×9-inch baking dish. Transfer hot cookies to powdered sugar. Roll cookies in powdered sugar, coating well. Let cookies cool in sugar in dish.

6 Sift remaining ½ cup powdered sugar over cookies just before serving. Store tightly covered at room temperature or freeze up to 1 month.

Makes about 4 dozen cookies

Pumpkin Roll

1 package (about 16 ounces) angel food cake mix

1¼ cups water

1¼ cups powdered sugar, divided

1 package (8 ounces) cream cheese, softened

1 container (8 ounces) whipped topping, thawed

½ cup solid-pack pumpkin

Cream Cheese Frosting (recipe follows)

½ cup chopped hazelnuts (optional)

1 Preheat oven to 350°F. Spray 17×12-inch jelly-roll pan with nonstick cooking spray. Line pan with waxed paper.

2 Beat cake mix and water according to package directions. Pour batter into prepared pan. Bake 17 minutes or until toothpick inserted into center comes out clean. Immediately invert cake onto clean towel sprinkled with ½ cup powdered sugar. Fold towel edge over cake edge and roll up cake and towel jelly-roll style into 12-inch-long roll. Place seam side down on wire rack to cool completely.

3 Beat cream cheese and remaining powdered sugar in large bowl with electric mixer at medium speed 2 minutes or until well blended and fluffy. Fold in whipped topping and pumpkin; refrigerate until ready to use. Prepare Cream Cheese Frosting.

4 Carefully unroll cake onto serving plate, removing towel. Spread pumpkin filling evenly over cake. Re-roll cake; place seam side down on plate. (If cake breaks, hold pieces together and roll as instructed. Breaks can later be hidden with frosting.) Frost with Cream Cheese Frosting; sprinkle with hazelnuts, if desired. Trim 1 inch off each end with serrated knife; discard scraps. Cover with plastic wrap; refrigerate 2 to 3 hours before serving.

Makes 10 servings

Cream Cheese Frosting

2 packages (8 ounces each) cream cheese, softened

½ cup (1 stick) butter, softened

2 cups powdered sugar, sifted

2 teaspoons vanilla

Beat cream cheese and butter with electric mixer at medium-high speed 2 minutes or until well blended and fluffy. Add powdered sugar and vanilla; beat well.

Death by Chocolate Poke Cake

1 package (about 15 ounces) dark chocolate cake mix, plus ingredients to prepare mix

1 cup semisweet chocolate chips

1 package (4-serving size) chocolate instant pudding and pie filling mix, plus ingredients to prepare mix

1 cup white chocolate chips

1 Prepare cake mix according to package directions; stir in chocolate chips. Bake cake according to package directions for 13×9-inch pan. Cool completely.

2 Poke holes in cake at ½-inch intervals with wooden skewer. Prepare pudding according to package directions. Pour pudding over cake. Top cake with white chocolate chips. Refrigerate 2 to 3 hours or until firm.

Makes 12 to 15 servings

Index

Metric Conversion Chart

VOLUME MEASUREMENTS (dry)

1/8 teaspoon = 0.5 mL
1/4 teaspoon = 1 mL
1/2 teaspoon = 2 mL
3/4 teaspoon = 4 mL
1 teaspoon = 5 mL
1 tablespoon = 15 mL
2 tablespoons = 30 mL
1/4 cup = 60 mL
1/3 cup = 75 mL
1/2 cup = 125 mL
2/3 cup = 150 mL
3/4 cup = 175 mL
1 cup = 250 mL
2 cups = 1 pint = 500 mL
3 cups = 750 mL
4 cups = 1 quart = 1 L

VOLUME MEASUREMENTS (fluid)

1 fluid ounce (2 tablespoons) = 30 mL
4 fluid ounces (1/2 cup) = 125 mL
8 fluid ounces (1 cup) = 250 mL
12 fluid ounces (1 1/2 cups) = 375 mL
16 fluid ounces (2 cups) = 500 mL

WEIGHTS (mass)

1/2 ounce = 15 g
1 ounce = 30 g
3 ounces = 90 g
4 ounces = 120 g
8 ounces = 225 g
10 ounces = 285 g
12 ounces = 360 g
16 ounces = 1 pound = 450 g

DIMENSIONS

1/16 inch = 2 mm
1/8 inch = 3 mm
1/4 inch = 6 mm
1/2 inch = 1.5 cm
3/4 inch = 2 cm
1 inch = 2.5 cm

OVEN TEMPERATURES

250°F = 120°C
275°F = 140°C
300°F = 150°C
325°F = 160°C
350°F = 180°C
375°F = 190°C
400°F = 200°C
425°F = 220°C
450°F = 230°C

BAKING PAN SIZES

Utensil	Size in Inches/Quarts	Metric Volume	Size in Centimeters
Baking or Cake Pan (square or rectangular)	8×8×2	2 L	20×20×5
	9×9×2	2.5 L	23×23×5
	12×8×2	3 L	30×20×5
	13×9×2	3.5 L	33×23×5
Loaf Pan	8×4×3	1.5 L	20×10×7
	9×5×3	2 L	23×13×7
Round Layer Cake Pan	8×1½	1.2 L	20×4
	9×1½	1.5 L	23×4
Pie Plate	8×1¼	750 mL	20×3
	9×1¼	1 L	23×3
Baking Dish or Casserole	1 quart	1 L	—
	1½ quart	1.5 L	—
	2 quart	2 L	—